Words to the Wise

A Lighthearted Look at the English Language

Michael J. Sheehan

www.Arbutuspress.com
Traverse City, Michigan

Sheehan, Michael 1939-
    Library of Congress Cataloging-in-Publication Data
Words to the Wise: a lighthearted look at the English Language / Michael J. Sheehan
    p. cm.
Includes index.
ISBN 0-9665316-8-X (pbk.)
1. English language —Usage. I. Title.

PE1460.S5176 2004
428—dc22
            2004008219

1 2 3 4 5 6 7 8 9 10

Cover design: Susan Bays

Cover illustration: Tim Gibbons
Illustration copyright © 2004 Tim Gibbons
tmgventuresinc@aol.com

To Dona, who knows my questions
before I ask them.

FOREWORD

Language is like the air we breathe: It's invisible. It's all around us. We can't get along without it, yet we take it for granted. But when we step back and really listen to the sounds and symbols that escape from the holes in people's faces, leak from their pens, and luminesce up on their computer screens, we experience the joy of lex.

Among languages, English is the most widely spoken in the history of our planet. English has acquired the largest and most cheerfully democratic vocabulary of all the world's languages. English is infinite in its variety, and so is Michael Sheehan. He is a word-happy, wordstruck, word- besotted, word-bethumped wordaholic, logolept, and verbivore. He is the English teacher you wish you had had. He is a fly-by-the roof-of-the-mouth user-friendly language guy at home in all matters linguistic—from puns to punctuation, pronouns to pronunciation, phrase origins to phraseology, and palindromes to philological palaver. Travel with this author-broadcaster-mentor on his joy ride through our glorious, uproarious, outrageous courageous, tremendous, stupendous, end-over endous English language and discover more than you have dreamt of in your philosophies about who you are and whence you have come.

Richard Lederer

April 2004

PREFACE

If someone were to walk into a station manager's office with a proposal for a radio call-in show about the English language that promised to answer questions about grammar, word choice, phrase origins, and the like—all the things we used to detest in Mrs. Smith's sixth grade class—he or she probably wouldn't be able to move fast enough to avoid the slamming door.

And yet, *Words to the Wise,* heard on WTCM (AM 580) every Tuesday morning at 9:00, is going into its third year in Traverse City, Michigan. It was the child of *Grammatically Incorrect,* with Ron Jolly and Steve Cook. I was a guest on their program several times after my *Word Parts Dictionary* was published in 2000. When Steve Cook decided to devote his time to other pursuits, I came aboard as a permanent guest, working for awhile with my broadcast mentor, John Dew, and now with Ron Jolly.

The popularity of the show is attested to by the volume of calls and e-mail that we receive. Part of it is due to the chemistry between Ron and me. He is intelligent, witty, and generous—a local icon in northern Michigan, as we teasingly call him. He makes it easy for me to focus on memory banks established while teaching for 26 years in the City Colleges of Chicago and while writing six other books. And we have fun.

Another large part of the program's success is a loyal and inquisitive audience. People from all walks of life, ranging in age from homeschoolers to senior citizens, call in with interesting questions. Sometimes it's an item they need to know for their job. Sometimes it's a puzzling word or phrase they have read in the newspaper or heard on television. Always, it's something for which they really want an answer, and I try to honor their authenticity and their need. The fact is, English is such a complicated language, and authorities are often so divided, that all of us feel a bit insecure at times.

That's why I wrote this book. The people who live in the Traverse City region are a microcosm of everyone else in the country. Their grammar and word choice questions are not unique; they are characteristic of the confusion and hesitancy that predominate today in writing and in speech. So before you plunge into the questions and answers that follow (taken from program transcripts and sometimes edited for the sake of clarity and brevity), allow me to utter the introduction that begins each show:

This is *Words to the Wise*, where grammar matters, spelling matters, and word choice matters—not because they're sacred cows, but because we need them to communicate accurately and securely. Our language is meant not to confine us, but to set us free. That's why the motto of this show is, "The limits of my language are the limits of my world." [*Ludwig Wittgenstein*]

Michael J. Sheehan
wordmall@aol.com

Also by Michael Sheehan

The Word Parts Dictionary (McFarland & Co., 2000)

Words! A Vocabulary Power Workbook (Harcourt Brace, 1996)

Handbook for Basic Writers (Prentice-Hall, 1991)

Workbook for Basic Writers (Prentice-Hall, 1991)

The Cry of the Jackal (Avalon Books, 1991)

In the Shadow of the Bear (Avalon Books, 1990)

Q. uestions

and

A. nswers

Q. I'm confused. Is it a *barefaced lie* or a *boldfaced lie*?

A. If you think you're confused now, try reading what the experts have to say. By the way, let me throw a third version into the mix: a *baldfaced* lie. All three are in actual use, although some stern souls say that *boldfaced* can refer only to **thick, heavy type**. Let's review a few sources.

The American Heritage Dictionary of Idioms endorses *barefaced lie*. At the same time, *The American Heritage Dictionary of the English Language*, 4th edition, gives a nod to *boldfaced lie* and *baldfaced lie*, with the implication that *barefaced lie* might work, too (all are defined as *brazen*).

Garner's Modern American Usage mentions that *baldfaced, barefaced,* and *boldfaced* are often used interchangeably to describe a lie, though *baldfaced* predominates.

This claim is contradicted by running a Google search using both hyphenated and non-hyphenated spellings for each term. On the day I ran a search, *bald (-)faced* had 29,360 hits, *bold (-)faced* had 81,250, and *bare (-)faced* garnered 122,110 hits—clearly, the popular winner.

The Oxford English Dictionary reveals that *boldfaced*, meaning impudent, showed up in print in 1590, and by 1712, *barefaced* had taken on the meaning of audacious or shameless. It doesn't even show *baldfaced* as a compound.

So here's what I think happened. The cliche´ started out as *a boldfaced lie*, impudence emphasized. It was later joined by *a barefaced lie*, undisguised contempt emphasized. And because a bare face is a hairless or bald face, *a baldfaced lie* showed up on the scene as a variation. Which one to use? You'll have allies in any case, but I think *barefaced* wins for euphony and frequency.

QUICK QUIZ
1. glossy black:

(A) pavonine (B) rutilant (C) piceous (D) helvine

Q. Where did the word hobo come from?

A. Why is it that no one asks me questions with easy, definitive answers? Explanations for this word wander all over the place, and tightly-held hierarchies abound. A bum is on the bottom of the social ladder and a tramp is slightly above. A hobo sees himself as better than these two, since he will work on occasion to sustain his travels. The most far-fetched explanation I've read is that it relates somehow to an oboe, because a wheedling voice begging for money has a reed-like quality. I've seen one or two hoboes in my day with harmonicas, but we're not talking traveling symphonic orchestras here. More likely is that it came from *hoe boy*, since a hobo may be viewed as a type of migrant worker. Another explanation is that it's a corruption of the friendly greeting *ho, boy!* or that it's a sarcastic rendition of *hey, beau*. Another suggestion is that soldiers returning home on foot after the Civil War were HOme BOund, but part of the essence of being a hobo is that he is homeless. The only agreement is that it was American in origin and that hoboes used the name in fellowship among themselves.

Q. Should it be "Tom is taller than I" or "Tom is taller than me"?

A. Here's another hot potato first cooked up by 18th century grammarians; they were a <u>most</u> contentious lot. Those who maintained that *than* is a conjunction went with the first version (*than I*), thus making *I* the subject of the understood verb *am*. Those who maintained that *than* is a preposition held out for the second version (*than me*), making *me* the object of a preposition. I think that most of us were taught that *than* is a conjunction, at least in formal situations, so we're always conjuring up latent verbs.

In our day, common sense makes it clear that either one could be correct given the right situation. Let's look at two sentences, both of which are correct:

- *Veronica hates Vince more than I.* This one really means, Veronica hates Vince more than I hate Vince.
- *Veronica hates Vince more than me.* The message here is, Veronica hates Vince more than she hates me.

The danger is that the subtle distinction may be lost on those who maintain a rigid position. The 300-year-old battle is still in progress. For a clear and sensible discussion, I recommend the article "Than" in *Merriam-Webster's Concise Dictionary of English Usage.*

Q.   Are colons and semicolons interchangeable?

A.   Don't you dare! The colon (:) acts as a pointer within a sentence. It points to a list or an explanation that expands on what has just been said. (*She admired two presidents above all: Lincoln and Truman.*) If you want to replace a colon, use a dash.

The semicolon (;) joins two independent clauses that are closely connected in meaning. (*The carpenter wielded the hammer; the apprentice held the nail.*) Since an independent clause is a full sentence all by itself, you could replace a semicolon with a period.

☞   BUMPER STICKER   ☜
A man's home is his castle, in a manor of speaking

Answer 1:
(C) piceous   [L. *pix*, pitch]

Many insects have piceous abdomens.

Q. Good writing is becoming rare in our region. A local golf course plasters this on its carts: "Children shall not drive golf carts under the age of 16." (So let them have the carts which are 17 and older.) An Italian delicatessen offers "Muscle Salad." (I guess it has a strong flavor.) And a news article reports, "As the knew man in the office, he felt overwhelmed." (*The Man Who Knew Too Much* revisited.)

A. It's not just this region. Probably because of unwarranted reliance on imperfect computer spell checkers, unintentional humor abounds. My favorite was the news report that told us that a local ne'er-do-well who was on the lamb (should be *lam*) had been captured. Boy, did he have a sheepish look when he was caught!

Q. I have to write field reports, and I must admit that I'm not the world's best writer. My supervisor says that if my reports were better organized, I'd get less criticism. How do I do that?

A. The three primary ways of organizing a paper or report are paying attention to time, space, and logical order. They can be mixed and matched depending on your topic.

Using time, you arrange events from what happened first, next, and last—or you can use reverse chronology. Be sure to sprinkle in lots of time signal words, such as *afterward, meanwhile, next, today, first, last,* and so on.

Using space, you describe an object or objects from left to right (or reverse), top to bottom, near to far, outside to inside, etc. Spatial signal words include *above, behind, center, down, near, north,* and *under.*

Using logical order, you must choose a single and clear method of arrangement. This might involve general to specific, large to small, less important to more important, familiar to unfamiliar, simple to complex, etc. Whichever method you choose, stick to it consistently. Move your facts and observations around so they fit the chosen pattern.

Q. I get very annoyed when I see people spelling Christmas as Xmas. I say, take the X out of Christmas!

A. I sympathize with you, but I think the spelling preferred by advertisers and headline writers is here to stay. By the way, the spelling is not as secular as you think. It's really a reflection of the Greek letter chi, the opening letter of χριστος, which we would spell as *Christ*. It means "the anointed one." Its root is shared by the word *christening*, which is used for everything from babies to battleships.

Q. I saw a sign in a fast-food joint which promised tasty French fry potatoes. Is that right?

A. Hmmm....what happened to the *-d* in Mickey D? It's wrong; the correct spelling is *fried*. I'm beginning to see this error in many places, often connected with food for some strange reason. Recent sightings include hot butter popcorn (buttered), cream spinach (creamed), a use car (used), can corn (canned), and distinguish writers (distinguished).

These are all adjectives formed from regular verbs, specifically from the past participle. Usually, they describe persons or things that are receivers of an action or process, and what they have received is basically completed. Something was done to them and they are changed. The *-d* ending adjective tells what kinds of persons or things they have become as a result of what happened to them. Consider the matter sign, seal, and deliver.

QUICK QUIZ
2. lacuna

(A) insect larva (B) a gap
(C) body of water (D) milky substance

Q.   Which is correct: *I clinched my teeth* or *I clenched my teeth*?

A.   Clenched. *Clinch* means to fix or secure; make final; in boxing, to grab. *They clinched the Division title in the final game of the season.* Oh, and two lip-locked lovers are *in a clinch.*

Clench means to close tightly; to grasp tightly. *I clenched my teeth; I clenched my fists; I clenched the steering wheel so hard that my knuckles turned white.*

Q.   Why do they call contradictory phrases (clean kill) oxymorons? That sounds like a name for stupid livestock.

A.   And that sounds like a very bad pun (paronomasia). In Greek, *oxy-* meant sharp intelligence, while *-moron* meant foolish stupidity. That's a very descriptive word for incongruous phrases. Here are some other examples:

current history

authentic reproduction

minor emergency

accurate stereotype

serious comedy

aggressive diplomacy

vacant dwelling

silent alarm

precise estimates

active retirement

small crowd

required option

loud whisper

uninvited guest

advanced beginner

detailed summary

rude welcome

non-stick glue

dry wine

ship by plane

plastic glasses

found missing

low speed

almost exactly

known secret

unlimited boundaries

rounded corners

Q. I'm getting married later this year, and the shop which will print our invitations gave me a book of typeface samples. Over and over, some kind of foreign phrase shows up as an illustration. I've copied it to send to you: *Lorem ipsum dolor sit amet, consectetur adipscing elit, diam nonnumy eiusmod tempor incidunt ut labore et dolo.* What language is this, and what does it say?

A. First of all, congratulations on your impending wedding. I trust that your printer will allow you to substitute your own names and information for the Latin sample. This is a printer's custom that goes back hundreds of years. Some unknown typesetter took a portion of Cicero's *de Finibus Bonorum et Malorum* (On the Purposes of Good & Evil), scrambled the sentences a bit, and started using it as text for a type sample book. The line now is jumbled into nonsense, but the original sentence from which it came spoke about the fact that no one pursues pain directly because it is desirable; it is always a by-product or consequence of some other pursuit.

Q. Is the expression "fit as a fiddle" due to the fact that a violin fits tightly under the musician's chin?

A. You might be able to make a case for that since no one is exactly sure of the origin. Today, the word *fit* means in good health. In 1616, when the phrase first shows up in print, it meant suitable. *Facts on File Encyclopedia of Word & Phrase Origins* suggests that a fiddle was considered fit (in good shape) because musicians took good care of their instruments

---

Answer 2: (B) a gap
[L. *lacuna*, hole]

The obvious lacuna in his story made the jury suspicious of his testimony.

---

in deference to their livelihood. *Brewer's Dictionary of Phrase & Fable* says it probably refers to the energetic swaying of street musicians. Robert Claiborne offers the observation that a fiddle which is correctly strung and carefully tuned is ready (suitable) for any piece the musician cares to play. Easy to string someone along with this one.

Q. Would it be *deficient* education or *defective* education?

A. That phrase normally shows up as *deficient education*. It means insufficient, incomplete, inadequate. In other words, there's not enough of something. On the other hand, there could be a defective education. This would happen when you learned everything offered about a given subject, but what you were taught was wrong. So the subtle distinction seems to be that something deficient is incomplete, while something defective, even though complete, is wrong or flawed.

Q. Where did the phrase "flash in the pan" come from? I say it's a photography term; my husband holds out for a military explanation.

A. It's military. A pan was the small cavity in the lock of a flintlock into which gun powder was poured. If the gunpowder burned off but didn't set off the charge, the result was flash and smoke, but no gunfire. It's true that early photographers used explosive flash powders to provide enough light for a picture, but guns—and this phrase—came long before then.

☞　　　WORD FACT　　　☜
The five most misspelled words in English are desiccate, minuscule, supersede, dumbbell and liquefy.

Q. Would you believe that this appeared in a college newspaper? "...our culture claims pride in such things as 50 Cent, Britney Spears, and Maxim, and all around us proud people pedal their ideas off as worthy of such standing." [*Cornell Daily Sun*, Oct. 30, 2003]

A. Having taught in a college for 26 years, I have no problem believing it at all. The writer should have written *peddle*, meaning to sell or to disseminate. Of course, if those proud people mentioned had been riding bicycles, the pedal would have come into play; and had they been strewing flowers, petals would be involved.

Q. I was the youngest child in my family, and my four siblings were boys. As you can imagine, I was the brunt of many cruel nicknames from my brothers Four-eyes, Dog Breath, Stumpy, and Baldy. But I've been wondering where the word *nickname* came from. Since a nick is defined as a notch or a cut, is it because these were cruel and cutting terms?

A. Not bad as speculation, but not every nickname is cruel. All states have nicknames, for instance, and governmental PR types try to make sure the names are tourist magnets. The American flag is affectionately known as Old Glory, and most people know where Big Ben is. To get back to the word itself, it's a variation on the original *a neke name*, which meant an additional (eke = also) name. At first, it seems to have been used for an incorrect name given to a person, but these days it can come from physical characteristics, actions, childish mispronunciations, affectionate variations, and so forth. You know you've turned a developmental corner when you select a nickname of <u>your</u> choice and make it stick.

QUICK QUIZ
3. mansuetude

(A) ferocity   (B) gentleness   (C) foresight   (D) ignorance

---

Q. Is there a real distinction between being dissatisfied and being unsatisfied?

A. There is a difference. *Dissatisfied* implies that something has been completed or has occurred, but the recipient or observer doesn't like the results. *Unsatisfied* implies that something was never completed or fulfilled; it fell short of the task. So if I finish a large dinner that featured overcooked and tasteless food, I am dissatisfied with the meal. If very small, but tasty, portions were served, my hunger may still be unsatisfied, though I am not dissatisfied with what I ate.

Q. Is persnickety a real word?

A. Any word that is or was in use is a real word, though it may not be proper in some contexts. It's a bit informal, so I wouldn't use it in a legal document, but it provides a colorful way to indicate that someone is fastidious or fussy or pretentious. It seems to have come from Scottish dialect. In its early 19th century form, it was spelled pernickety.

Q. Here's a contribution to your Museum of Headline Horrors: "Iraq and Syria warned to reign in Hezbollah"

A. Ah, the old royal treatment. Here's another instance where the spellchecker is *not* your best friend. Three legitimate words share the same pronunciation but must maintain separate spellings. The headline should have used *rein in*, meaning to check or hold back. It's an obvious reference to a rider reining in a horse. *Reign* is the word used of kings and queens, and *rain* means precipitation.

Hey, I'm in charge; don't reign on my parade.

Q. For a feature article, I need to know the name for a person who's an expert on ferns.

A. That would be a pteridologist. It comes from a Greek word that meant wing. Certain ferns do look like a bird's wing, so we can see why that root was used. Connected words include pteridomania (an enthusiasm for ferns) and pteridoid (shaped like a fern). If you ever have occasion to pronounce the word, remember that the **p** is silent.

Q. What's the difference between a malapropism and a spoonerism?

A. First, their similarities: they both involve word mangling, and they are eponyms—they come from a person's name. Malapropism was named after Mrs. Malaprop, a character in Richard Sheridan's 1775 comedy, *The Rivals*. Poor Mrs. Malaprop always confused similar-sounding words: As headstrong as an allegory (alligator) on the banks of the Nile; French Prevential (Provincial) furniture; you must illiterate (obliterate) that from your memory. Clergyman and educator William Spooner lent his name—thanks to his students— to the type of error where letters are transposed: "occupewing a pie" for occupying a pew; "ears and sparrows" for spears and arrows; "May I sew you to another sheet?" for May I show you to another seat? Both errors should remind us of that old maxim: Spink before you theak.

Answer 3: (B) gentleness
[L. *mansuetus*, tame]

While mansuetude is a desirable spiritual goal, it won't impress the neighborhood bully.

Q. Do you happen to know the only 15 letter word that does not repeat letters within the word? The word is uncopyrightable, and was a quiz item on a radio program.

A. A word that repeats no letters is known as an isogram, but according to *Wordplay,* by Chris Cole, there is one other word with 15 unrepeated letters: dermatoglyphics. And ambidextrously has 14 separate letters.

Q. When should I use brackets and when parentheses in writing reports?

A. Brackets are the square enclosure marks inserted by a second writer to signal corrections, interposed comments, explanatory notes, or translations that were not in the original text.

Parentheses are the rounded enclosure marks used primarily to signal definitions, examples, and other remarks by the original writer of the text. Use parentheses sparingly. (Too many of them indicate that you are getting wordy and drifting away from the main point.)

<u>Helpful Hint</u>: Enclosing the word *sic,* meaning *thus,* in brackets [sic] is a way of signaling to the reader, "Don't blame *me* for the misspelling or factual error; that's the way I found it in the original."

Q. I'd like to know where the phrase *rule of thumb* came from. I remember reading it had something to do with being permitted to beat your wife with a rod no thicker than your thumb. Is this correct?

A. It makes for an incendiary story, but no—that's a piece of folk etymology. The phrase refers to the use of rough and ready practical experience rather than formal procedures in getting something done. It's most likely that the saying comes from carpenters using the length of the first joint of the thumb, which is about an inch long, to measure things. So "rule" refers to a ruler in the sense of measurement, not of despotism or male chauvinism.

Other parts of the body were used as a ruler, too. A foot was determined by a pace, the distance from the tip of the nose to the outstretched fingers is roughly a yard, and horse heights are still measured by hands—the width of the palm and closed thumb is about four inches. For a lengthy discussion, check out Michael Quinion's *World Wide Words* at www.quinion.com/words/

Q.   In yesterday's newspaper, a California judge who didn't believe a witness was quoted as saying, "That's incredulous!" Time for order in the court?

A.   The jury is in on this one. What we have here is the *incredible/incredulous* dichotomy. Only a person can be incredulous within himself or herself, meaning disbelieving. An external event or statement can be incredible, that is, not worthy of belief. So the judge should have said, "That's incredible, and I'm incredulous!" Note the common root, *-cred-*. It shows up in many words, and it refers to belief.

☞ THE GAME OF THE NAME ☜
Agnes comes from the Latin for lamb

QUICK QUIZ
4. equivocate:

(A) to mean the same (B) to ride a horse
(C) to lie (D) to furnish with tools

Q. I heard a consultant on CNN refer to some Taliban leader as *beyond the pail*. What does this mean? Is he getting ready to kick the bucket?

A. Most of your confusion comes from thinking that the word **pale** is spelled **p-a-i-l**. It actually has nothing to do with a bucket. The meaning of the phrase is, *beyond acceptable conduct, outside civilized society or limits*. **Pale** comes from the Latin *palum*, a stake or pointed stick. In England, it came to mean a fence around a territory that was under a particular authority, such as a cathedral pale or a village pale. Inside the pale, things were orderly and regulated. Outside the pale, there could be disorder and lack of political jurisdiction.

Q. What's the difference between a proverb and an adage?

A. Not much. Both are brief expressions of generally accepted truths.

PROVERBS are short, pithy statements of practical wisdom. (*As the door turns upon its hinge, so turns the sluggard upon his bed.* <u>Proverbs</u> 26:14) ADAGES are time-honored proverbs, almost clichés. (*Actions speak louder than words.*) And the following terms are close in meaning.

MAXIM: succinct expression of a practical rule of conduct. (*Neither a borrower nor a lender be.* <u>Hamlet</u>)

EPIGRAM: a witty expression or observation. (*Remarriage is the triumph of hope over experience.* Samuel Johnson)

APHORISM: a tersely stated saying. (*Early to bed and early to rise makes a man healthy, wealthy and wise.* <u>Poor Richard's Almanack</u>)

PLATITUDE: a trite saying, especially if presented as a fresh thought. (*The early bird gets the worm.*)

DICTUM: an authoritative, often formal pronouncement. (*If you understand it, it is not God.* Augustine of Hippo)

APOTHEGM: a terse, witty, instructive saying; a maxim. (*There is nothing in this world constant except inconstancy.* Swift)

Q. My wife cringes every time we're approached by a street person looking for a handout; she's genuinely afraid. Is there a word for this?

A. You are describing **ptochophobia**, the fear of beggars. The -*phobia* part of the word comes from a Greek word meaning fear or strong aversion. The *ptocho-* combining form also comes from ancient Greek, this time a word meaning a poor person or beggar. It's certainly not a common word part today, but the *Oxford English Dictionary* also lists ptochocracy (the poor as a class), ptochogony (the begetting of beggars), and ptochology (scientific study of poverty, unemployment, etc.). A useful word in a recession.

An aside: I wonder if this word part was the source of *petaQ*, an insult hurled by Klingons on the *Star Trek* series. Any evidence out there?

Q. What's the most frequent mistake that you encounter?

A. With no hesitation, I'd say switched homonyms—words that sound alike but are not spelled alike. Chief among these are *their/there/they're*, *it's/its*, *two/too/to*, and *your/you're*. And even in this day of spellcheckers in word processing programs, they slip by constantly because all are authentic words, and the checker isn't sophisticated enough to factor in context. Its two bad that their such a problem.

Answer 4: (C) to lie
[L. *equi-*, equal + *vocare*, to call]

Because he was known to equivocate, he was not chosen as a police informant.

Q. The store where I shop has two signs next to each other at the checkout counter: "12 items or less" and "12 items or fewer." What's going on?

A. Sounds like an insecure manager to me. The general rule for the difference between *less* and *few/fewer* is this: (1) Use *few/fewer* to describe things that can be counted—*fewer cigarettes, fewer cars, fewer jobs.* (2) Use *less* to describe things that cannot be counted—*less smoking, less traffic, less employment.* So "12 items or fewer" is correct.

However, to be fair, in idiomatic English—and more and more in formal usage—*less* is being used with a plural noun denoting **time, amount, or distance**: *There are less than two minutes to play in the game; She makes less than $40,000 a year; We have less than three miles to go.* In other words, sometimes separate, countable elements (which would therefore need the word *fewer*) are treated as an unbroken unit and the word *less* is then acceptable. Until the dust settles, play it safe and follow the rules in paragraph one.

Q. A spelling bee list printed in our newspaper contained the word ponerology, but it didn't give definitions. I can't find this word in my dictionary.

A. You'll have to use an unabridged dictionary, perhaps at your local library. Ponerology is a branch of theology; basically, it's the study of evil. It comes from a Greek word (*poneiros*) which means wicked. The *-logy* ending signifies "a study of..." I wonder what kind of homework the teacher gives in a ponerology class.

☞   WORD FACT   ☜
Many people believe there are no words that rhyme with orange, purple, and silver, but we have sporange (a sporecase), curple (a rump), and chilver (a lamp).

Q. I read on the internet that *fired,* meaning dismissed from a job (*he was fired*) came about in the 18th century when landowners burned down tenants' houses rather than pay taxes on occupied land.

A. The internet probably has more language myths than realities, and this is one of them. The *Oxford English Dictionary* tells us that fired in this sense is American slang. It means "To turn (anyone) out of a place; to eject or expel forcibly; to dismiss or discharge peremptorily; to reject (a picture sent in for exhibition). Frequently with *out.*"

1885: "If the practice is persisted in, then pupils should be fired out."

1887: "Postmaster Breed says the next time such a thing occurs he will fire the offender bodily."

The context here suggests firing from a cannon rather than torching a house. *Discharge* shares the same duality: it refers to firing a gun and firing someone from a job.

Q. I'm having trouble with quotation marks. It's not so much the quotation marks themselves, it's the other marks that go with them. Is there any simple rule that I can follow?

A. There are three short rules that will keep you out of trouble; they all apply to the 2nd, or ending, quotation mark, not to the 1st one.

QUICK QUIZ
5. gulosity:

(A) pride (B) gluttony (C) lust (D) thievery

---

1. Periods and commas go **inside** the last quotation mark. "If you ask me," she said, "he can't be trusted."
2. Colons and semicolons go **outside** the last quotation mark. He promised, "I will not raise taxes"; the voters did not believe him.
3. Question marks and exclamation points go **inside** the last quotation mark when they apply to the quoted material, but **outside** when they apply to the whole sentence. "What would you like to drink—tea or coffee?" asked the waiter. Who said, "Give me liberty or give me death"?

Q.   The word "news" did not come about because it was the plural of "new." It came from the first letters of the words North, East, West and South. This was because information was being gathered from all different directions. True?

A.   Word authorities disagree with this. When the word news first showed up in English meaning "tidings" or "report" as it does now, it wasn't even spelled n-e-w-s. Inconsistent spelling was normal and unremarkable before the 18th century.

Thus, 1423: "I bring the **newis** glad..."
1485: "Yet of late I have hard [sic] no **newys**."
1523: "He was sore troubled with those **newes**."

News <u>was</u> the plural form of *new*. It came from the Old French term *novele*, which came ultimately from the Latin *novum*, new. [*Source: Oxford English Dictionary*]

Q.   I thought there was supposed to be a difference in meaning between *flaunt* and *flout*, but they seem to be blending these days. What happened?

A.   Ignorance happpened. To *flaunt* is to show off: you flaunt your new necklace by wearing it to work. If you've got it, flaunt it. Pride or ostentation is involved. *Flout* has a more negative and antisocial connotation. It means to treat some rule or standard with contempt. Clichés include "to flout convention" or "to flout the law." Scorn is an element.

Q. I want to share a word that I heard on the Discovery Channel. In a program about bats, the narrator called some of them fructivorous, which means feeding on fruit, and I think that's a great word.

A. I agree, and I thank you for reminding us of this useful adjective. That last part (*-vorous*) comes from the Latin term *vorare*, to devour, and the *fructi-* part comes from the Latin word for fruit. Food is so important to all living things that you'll find 40 or 50 words ending in *–vorous*. Among them are carnivorous (flesh-eating), omnivorous (eating everything), and herbivorous (eating plants). Less well known are apivorous (eating bees), formicivorous (eating ants), merdivorous (eating dung), oryzivorous (eating rice), and vermivorous (eating worms). If we play with the root, we could also come up with BigMacivorous.

Q. A major bookstore chain sent me this in an e-mail: "Enjoy our fast and free gift wrapping service. We have several attractive designs from which you may choose. Compliment the perfect present with the perfect presentation!"

A. Ah, the dreaded **compliment/complement** pair. A **compliment** is an expression of praise, admiration or congratulations. **Complement** means to complete or bring to perfection. So, for instance, we would compliment the chef

---

Answer 5: (B) gluttony
[L. *gula*, throat]

"They are very temperate, seldom offending in ebriety, nor erring in gulosity...." Sir Thomas Browne

---

because he created a dessert that was the perfect complement to a meal. The ad should have read, "*complement* the perfect present...."

Q. I can't always tell which word to use, continual or continuous. What's the difference?

A. Contrary to what many people think, **continual/ continually** and **continuous/continuously** are not synonyms.

- Continual = recurring regularly or frequently; with breaks. *They are continually holding noisy parties, causing the neighbors to call the police.*
- Continuous = uninterrupted; occurring without a break. *The continuous ticking of the clock kept me awake all night.*

Of the two, *continuous* is more frequently misused: *To get what they want, dogs will **continuously** scratch, bark, whine, and stare.* [Should be *continually.*] Our congregation's living creche scene has been held **continuously** *since 1963.* [Should be *annually,* unless those actors have iron bladders.]

Think of the *-ual* at the end of *continual* as a mnemonic for *Until A Letup.* A continual event is intermittent and will always have a letup or break.

Q. I get confused by capital letters. I have noticed that the very same word sometimes gets capitalized and sometimes doesn't. What gives?

A. To sort this out, you need to distinguish between two kinds of nouns. A **proper noun** is the name of a particular person, place, or thing. Your own name is an example of a proper noun. A **common noun** is a generic name; it does not refer to a particular individual. It's the difference between "Traverse City" and "a city in northern Michigan."

The overall rule is this: Capitalize proper nouns; do not capitalize common nouns.

Proper Noun	Common Noun
Munson Boulevard	the boulevard next to the lake
Lake Michigan	We swam in the lake.
The Paul Bunyon Building	the building next door
Governor Granholm	the governor of this state

Exception: The first word of a sentence must be capitalized even if it is a common noun.

Peripheral: (1) Don't capitalize a common noun after internal punctuation (such as a comma or colon or dash or semicolon) unless a direct quote follows. (2) In titles, capitalize the important words; don't capitalize prepositions, articles, and coordinating conjunctions unless they are the first or last words of the title.

Q.   Snot isn't a real word, is it?

A.   But if it's snot, what is? Slang words or dialectical terms *are* real words, even if they don't fit comfortably in all social situations. Besides, snot (meaning mucus) has been spelled that way since Middle English (along with *snotte*), and derives from the Old English word *gesnot*.

An interesting sidebar: did you ever notice how many words relating to the nose begin with the letters *s-n-* ? We have snout, snuffle, snort, snuff, sniffle, snoot, snootful, sniv-

---

QUICK QUIZ
6. adaptable:

(A) febrile   (B) ductile   (C) labile   (D) puerile

---

elling, sneeze, snub, snot, snot-rag, and snotcicle. It's no accident. There's an Indo-European root *snu-* that is responsible for many "nose" words (the ones just listed, plus terms such as schnoz and schnauzer). Nobody nose the trouble I've seen.

Q. Isn't "close proximity" a redundancy? I found it in a newspaper column.

A. Good eye. For the uninitiated, a redundancy is an excessively wordy or repetitious expression, such as refer back (refer), continue on (continue), and cooperate together (cooperate). Other examples are red in color (red), triangular in shape (triangular), large in size (large), protest against (protest), exact same (same), end result (result), new recruit (recruit), and final outcome (outcome).

Q. Is there a name for single words which have multiple and contradictory meanings? For instance, **apparent** can mean "unclear and dubious" (*He is the apparent winner, but there will be a recount*), but it can also mean "clear and unmistakable" (*Her intelligence is apparent in everything she does*).

A. Charles Ellis <http://www-personal.umich.edu/~cellis/antagonym.html> calls these words **antagonyms**, a word he constructed from *antagonize* (to counteract) and the combining form *–onym* (word or term). Richard Lederer coined another word in his 1989 book, *Crazy English*. He used the term **contronyms** to describe words with contradictory meanings. Whichever name one prefers, such words are fascinating to study. Here's a sample:
- **bound**:1. moving (*I was bound for Chicago.*)
            2. unable to move (*His arms were bound behind him.*)
- **clip**: 1. to attach (*Clip the coupon to your sales receipt.*)

2. to cut off (*Clip the hedges before you leave for the beach.*)

- **dust**: 1. to remove dust (*She dusted each figurine on the table.*)

  2. to apply dust (*The detectives dusted the apartment for prints.*)

- **left**: 1. still here (*Fred is the only one left.*)

  2. gone (*Fred left during the intermission.*)

- **mad**: 1. attracted to (*She is mad about the boy.*)

  2. repulsed by (*He makes her so mad that she sputters.*)

Q. What's the rule for adding an apostrophe to words such as *ours* or *hers* ?

A. The rule is simple: **don't do it!** All the rules about using apostrophes to show possession apply to nouns or to word groups acting as nouns. When it comes to pronouns, which is what *ours* and *hers* are, the rules for possession change. Memorize this list: *yours, his, hers, its, ours, theirs*. They NEVER take an apostrophe to show possession. Their spelling <u>already</u> shows possession.

Q. Is there a difference between noxious and obnoxious?

A. Both words are based on a root that means harmful, that *–nox-* letter combination. **Noxious** means "physically harmful or destructive to living beings" or it can mean "mor-

---

Answer 6: (C) labile
[L. *labi-*, apt to slip]

He is an emotionally labile person.

---

ally corrupting." *Noxious chemical waste; noxious ideas.* The focus, I would say, is on the harmful object itself; no observer need be present. **Obnoxious**, on the other hand, subtly shifts the focus to the viewer, the one who reacts. It betrays feelings of aversion or disgust. *His behavior was obnoxious.* "To me" or "to anyone watching" invariably seems to be implied.

Q. When you're trying to show possession with an apostrophe and an -s, how do you know whether to place the apostrophe before or behind the -s?

A. Some textbooks get into all the technicalities involved in this question and launch into discussions about singular and plural nouns, about common and proper nouns, about monosyllabic and polysyllabic nouns, or about the quality of a word-final –s sound. Let's make it simple and focus on just two rules:

- (1) If the word showing possession does NOT end in the letter –s, add an apostrophe + s.

  car + engine = car's engine
  dog + loyalty = dog's loyalty

- (2) If the word showing possession already ends in the letter –s, add only an apostrophe.

  ladies + coats = ladies' coats
  Ross + house = Ross' house

If you follow these rules, expect that some people will call it oversimplification. If you feel the need to justify yourself, you may refer to *The Handbook for Basic Writers*, published by Prentice-Hall, or to *The Beacon Handbook*, published by Houghton Mifflin.

Q. Is there a connection between autobiography and autopsy, or are the opening letters just an accident?

A. Well, a book critic might dissect an autobiography.... Enough! Both words share the same combining form, which means "self." Autopsy may be translated as "seeing for yourself." The difference between a biography and an autobiography is whether you wrote your own life story, or someone else did. And isn't it strange that autopsies have become a favorite theme on television shows, as witness *CSI* and its offspring and *Crossing Jordan*, among others. I guess it's a lively subject after all.

Q. I came across this dubious usage the other day: "This begs the question, will massive tax cuts really help the economy?" Isn't this a distortion of a term in logic?

A. No question about it. Many writers seem to think that "begging the question" is the same as "raising the question"; it's not. Begging the question means *assuming* the truth of what's supposed to be proved, as in "Since I never lie, it's obvious that I'm telling the truth." Another example: "God exists because the Bible says so, and He wrote the Bible, so it can't be wrong." Instead of offering proof, it simply restates, or mirrors, what has already been said. Solid conclusions are based on evidence, not on synonyms. This is also known as circular reasoning. Like a dog chasing its own tail, it runs in circles and gets nowhere.

QUICK QUIZ
7. faucal: pertaining to

(A) the face (B) the ribs (C) the throat (D) the kidney

Q. Why do we have an outbreak of Centres in Traverse City instead of Centers?

A. What we have here is the difference between American and British spelling. The American version would be *Center*; the British version is *Centre*. Another difference shows up in the American and British spellings of the word *theater* (American) and *theatre* (British). So the endings **–er** or **-re** mark one spelling difference between Brits and Yanks. Another is the **–or/-our** variation. This appears in words such as *honor/honour, labor/labour, behavior/behaviour* and *color/colour*. And then there's the **–og/-ogue** variation, which is most commonly found in *catalog/catalogue* or *monolog/monologue*.

We may blame Noah Webster for the disparity. In his *Dissertations on the English Language* (1789), he proposed the institution of an "American Standard" of spelling, partly for patriotic reasons, and partly to simplify spelling by eliminating unpronounced letters. His *American Spelling Book*—first published in 1783 and popular for over 60 years (it sold a million copies a year in the 1850s)—and his *American Dictionary of the English Language* (1828), produced a distinctly American spelling.

Webster proposed some radical spelling changes that never caught on. He would have changed *bread* to *bred* and *feather* to *fether*, for instance, and *grief* would have been spelled *greef*. He would have dropped all final e's, as in *definit* and *examin*, *isle* would have been *ile*, and *tongue* would have been *tung*.

So as long as people mistakenly think that British spelling has more class, we'll see a lot of Centres in town.

☞   BUMPER STICKER   ☜
A pessimist's blood type is always b-negative

Q. Is the word *brainwashing* always negative in its connotation? I need to know if it's an undesirable word to use when speaking of religious education.

A. That depends on whether you're for it or against it. The word came from the Mandarin Chinese (*xi nao*, to wash the brain). It still refers to forcible indoctrination aimed at destroying a person's beliefs and replacing them with an alternative set of fixed beliefs. Over time, the secondary meaning has softened a bit, so that it now also refers to a concentrated form of persuasion, such as an intense ad campaign. But it's still negative.

So when speaking positively of religious education, you might want to use the word *catechize*—to teach religious beliefs by means of questions and answers. The root of the word means to teach by word of mouth, and allied words are catechism, catechist, and catechesis. A couple of other religious teaching words are *evangelize*, to preach the Gospel [Gk. *eu angelos*, good news] and *kerygma*, the proclamation of religious truths [Gk. *kerugma*, preaching; herald].

In a secular setting, you have available words such as *instruct, persuade, influence,* and *affect.* Save the word *brainwashing* as an insult.

☞   WORD FACT   ☜

English is used all over the world in various professions (aviation, for instance), but if you estimate the number of people who speak English as their native language, it comes out to about 330 million. In contrast, about 750 million people claim Mandarin Chinese as their first language.

Answer 7: (C) the throat
[L. *faux*, throat]

The Semitic alphabets possess a notation for the
faucal breaths. (Isaac Taylor)

Q. I sometimes have problems with a pair of opposites: good/well and bad/badly. Do you have a shortcut?

A. You are not alone. That's the good news. The bad news is that you have to know the difference between an adjective and an adverb to use those words correctly.

1. An adjective is a word that describes or limits a noun or noun substitute; normally, it answers the questions *what kind, how many,* or *which one.*

2. An adverb describes or limits verbs, adjectives, or other adverbs; normally, it answers the questions *how, how much, how often, where, when,* or *why.*

- *Good* describes someone or something; it is an adjective. So is *bad.*
- *Well* describes an action or condition; it is an adverb. So is *badly.*

  My grandfather drives his motorcycle *well*; he is a *good* driver.

  My grandfather drives his motorcycle *badly*; he is a *bad* driver.

  Fresh air is *good*; polluted air is *bad.*

  This air filter works *well*; that air filter works *badly.*

COMPLICATIONS:

1. *feels, seems, tastes, appears* used as linking verbs (substituting for "is") require an adjective right after the verb.

2. *Well* is also used as an adjective to mean *healthy*: she isn't well. Study these examples:

  He appears to be *good* (not evil). He appears to be *well* (not unhealthy).

  She feels *bad* about your loss. (describes *she*, not *feels*)

She feels *badly* ever since her fingertips were burned; she can no longer distinguish items by touch. (describes *feels*, not *she*)

I feel *good* (describes *I*).

I feel *well*. (Could describe *I*, a health issue, or could describe *feel*, a reference to fingertip nerve endings.

Q. What is an aptronym?

A. Aptronym is a word coined by Franklin P. Adams for a name that is aptly suited to its owner. In the Traverse area, we find a pediatrician named Dr. Small, an obstetrician named Dr. Bump, a psychologist named Dr. Love, and lawyers with last names of Anger, Robb, Risk, Law, and Justice. Nationally, we find Peter Hammer (hardware store clerk), Nita House (real estate agent), Ken Lawless (police chief), Cathy Book (bookstore clerk), and Leonard Divine (rabbi).

For more examples, see
http://www.m-w.com/lighter/name/aptronym.htm

Q. I'm not always sure when to put quotation marks around a statement, and this annoys my boss, who's a freelance writer and motivational speaker. Can you help?

A. Perhaps the problem is not knowing the difference between a direct quote and an indirect quote. A *direct quote* uses the exact words of another speaker or writer, and it en-

---

QUICK QUIZ
8. humorous or playful teasing:

(A) cozenage (B) empennage (C) pannage (D) badinage

---

closes those words in quotation marks. An *indirect quote* gives a report, a rewording of what someone else said or wrote, and it does **not** use quotation marks.

"Where can I buy a good used car?" asked Henry.
Henry asked where he could buy a good used car.
"I enjoy books," she explained, "as well as magazines."
She explained that she enjoys books as well as magazines.
"You have lost your boyish good looks," said his wife.
His wife complained that he had lost his boyish good looks.

Q. One of the strangest terms that I've seen recently is anatonym, defined as a part of the body used as a verb. Are you familiar with this?

A. Yes. I don't know who invented the term, but I know that Richard Lederer included it in *Crazy English*. He gives to *toe* the line, *foot* the bill, and *face* the music as examples. Other instances include to *finger* a suspect, *hand* down a verdict, *palm* something off, *thumb* your nose, *nose* into someone's business, *eye* someone, *elbow* your way, *shoulder* your way, *head* an organization, and *stomach* bad news.

An aside: I can't tell you how many times I've received email that starts off, "English is a crazy language. In what other language do people drive in a parkway and park in a driveway?" Later, it will read, "If the plural of *tooth* is *teeth*, shouldn't the plural of *booth* be *beeth*?" No one gives the proper attribution, a legal and an ethical requirement. It wasn't written by Anonymous and it wasn't written by the sender. Give credit for this imaginative essay to Richard Lederer and *Crazy English* (1989).

☞ THE GAME OF THE NAME ☜
Anna comes from a Hebrew word meaning favor or grace

Q. What's the difference between *amount* and *number*?

A. I will admit that the distinction is getting blurred, but it's still useful to keep them separate. Use *amount* when you're referring to non-count nouns, nouns that are viewed as a single entity and don't normally have a plural: *an excessive amount of anger, an inadequate amount of guilt, an appropriate amount of caution.* Use *number* with count nouns, nouns that can have a plural: *a number of negative emotions, a growing number of marriages, a startling number of books.* A large amount of rules can lead to a growing number of confusion, eh?

Q. Should I write *advanced notice* or *advance notice* when I ask customers to sign up for news of upcoming sales?

A. **Advance notice** is correct. Think of it this way: *advance* means ahead of time, earlier than other people. *Advanced* means sophisticated or complex, at a higher level, and has nothing to do with early warning. Thus, you may get advance notification of a technologically advanced cell phone.

☞ WORD FACT ☜

The combination -ough can be pronounced eight different ways: "A rough-coated, dough-faced, thoughtful ploughman strode through the streets of Scarborough; after falling into a slough, he coughed and hiccoughed."

Answer 8: (D) badinage
[Fr. *badiner*, to joke]

The guests at the banquet engaged in playful badinage, thus adding to the enjoyment.

Q. Our neighborhood association meets every two months. Should we call them bimonthly or semimonthly meetings in the newsletter?

A. Many people are confused by these terms. Traditionally in this situation, *bi-* signifies "every two..." and *semi-* signifies "twice a ...."

- Biweekly = every two weeks; semiweekly = twice a week
- Bimonthly = every two months; semimonthly = twice a month
- Biennial = every two years; semi-annual = twice a year.

Knowing that most people will be confused by these distinctions, perhaps you should speak of meeting every two months or twice a month.

Q. How did "sent up the river" come to mean going to jail?

A. You've been watching James Cagney movies on late-night TV again. It refers to Sing Sing Prison in Ossining, New York. It is north of New York City on the Hudson River—hence, up the river in a most literal sense. And littoral, come to think of it.

Q. What does it mean when someone says, "That's a Catch-22"?

A. Contrary to what many people think, it's not just a barrier or a bump along the way. It's a circular trap from which there is **no** escape. The phrase comes from Joseph Heller's novel *Catch 22*. The dilemma was this: an airman who was crazy could be grounded; all he had to do was ask. But if he did ask, he was considered sane because obviously he realized the dangers of combat. He might be crazy to fly more missions and sane if he didn't, but if he was sane, he had to fly. In other words, there was no way out: crazy or sane, you *had* to fly the combat missions. Great novel, by the way.

Q. When do I use toward and towards?

A. As far as usage goes, Americans favor *toward* and the British prefer *towards*. Other than that, they are interchangeable.

Q. When I read between the lines to get someone's message, am I *implying* or *inferring*?

A. You are inferring. Think of it as a matter of direction. If you are sending out an indirect message (a tone of voice or a look, for instance), you are *implying*. If you are receiving (deciphering) a hint, you are *inferring*. I am told, however, that in the legal profession the lines are occasionally blurred. But outside of court, mind your directions.

Q. I always thought that the phrase "a wolf in sheep's clothing" came from an old fable, but my uncle says that it comes from the Bible. Who's right?

A. Not to appear sheepish, but I'd say you both are.
The Wolf in Sheep's Clothing is the name of a fable by Aesop, who lived in the 6th century B.C. His point: appearances are deceptive. The same idea shows up in Matthew 7:15, which warns, "Beware of false prophets, who come to you in sheep's

---

QUICK QUIZ
9. etiolated

(A) pale & sickly (B) ethical (C) elegant (D) confused

---

clothing, but inwardly are ravening wolves." It's a graphic and enduring figure of speech. For instance, a recent search on Google revealed about 44,000 hits for the phrase "sheep's clothing."

Q. Evidently, the mispronunciation "prostrate gland" didn't die out with Archie Bunker; I still hear it, even on television news. What's your comment?

A. I bow down before the wisdom of your observation; I prostrate myself. Listen up, guys: what you possess is a prostate gland—only one *r*. To prostrate is to lie face down. So you might have to prostrate yourself on the examination table for a thorough prostate exam, but they're not the same thing.

Q. When someone is being evasive, why do we call it *waffling*? Is it like batter sputtering on a griddle?

A. That's a very imaginative suggestion, but unlike wafflebutt (someone who sits all day and gets creases from a cane chair), it has nothing to do with food. Instead, it comes from *waff*, an old British dialectical word that imitated the sound of a barking dog. So to waffle is to yap.

Q. Why do we say "Wend-z-day" but spell it Wednes-day?

A. Originally, in an earlier form of English, it was a variant of Woden's day, Woden being a Germanic god. In fact, all the days of the week were named after Germanic gods or cosmic objects.

- Sunday: the day of the sun.
- Monday: the day of the moon.
- Tuesday: the day of the war god Tiu.

- Wednesday: the day of Woden, swift messenger god.
- Thursday: the day of Thor, lord of the sky.
- Friday: the day of Frig, goddess of love.
- Saturday: the day of Saturn, god of agriculture.

Q. What about giving me the Eagle-Eye Award of the Week? I found the following errors: "Leelanau County acts as host for hoards of people on vacation," and "These people make you want to gag, wretch, and hurl."

A. If we had such an award, it would be in the mail right now. This alert reader caught *hoards* (hidden funds or supplies) being used instead of the correct *hordes* (swarms or crowds). In the second example, *wretch* (a miserable person) incorrectly replaced *retch* (try to vomit).

Q. Which is correct: "My sister who lives in Flint is a lawyer" or "My sister, who lives in Flint, is a lawyer." In other words, should I use commas or not?

A. Here's a great example of why punctuation was invented. The first sentence (without commas) tells the reader that you have *more than one* sister. The second sentence (with commas) tells the reader that you have *only one* sister. Leaving the commas out makes the clause restrictive; it's needed to pinpoint which sister because you have more than one. (*My sister who lives in Flint*, as opposed to *my other sister who*

Answer 9: (A) pale, sickly
[OF *esteule* < L. *stipula*, stalk]
(Think of a plant without sunlight.)
After decades of incarceration, the prisoner's
face was etiolated.

---

lives in Petoskey.) Putting the commas in makes the clause nonrestrictive; it could just as well have been left out because it contains extra, not necessary, information.

There's a message here: even the lowly comma can be important. Don't slip into a coma when it comes to punctuation.

Q. Last Sunday, my pastor used this line in his sermon: "Because of their temerity, the Apostles did not come to Jesus' aid." Shouldn't that be timidity?

A. You're correct. Temerity means boldness, reckless courage. Since your pastor was speaking of fear, he should have said timidity. We'll have to charge him with a venial sin.

Q. Can you say something about words which sound alike but have different spellings, and words which are spelled alike but have different meanings?

A. There are actually three variations here, word sets with certain similarities as well as differences.

Focusing on the similarities, we have homographs, homonyms, and homophones.

(1) A homograph [from Greek *homo-*, same, and *–graph*, something written] is a word spelled the same as another, but having a different meaning, derivation, or pronunciation.

lead (led / leed)
He used a lead pencil to lead the orchestra.

bow (boe / baugh)
She tied a bow to the bow of the ship.

entrance (enTRANCE / ENtrens)
I was entranced by the ornate entrance.

44

When we focus on the differences, it is called a heterograph.

(2) A homonym [from Greek *homo-*, same, and *–nym*, name] is a word spelled and sounding the same as another, but having a different meaning and origin.

pool
The pool table was located near the swimming pool.
The neighbors pooled their money for the football pool.

bank
They slid down the bank into the river.
Don't forget to put your check in the bank.
She approached a bank of elevators.
We flew through a cloud bank.
Don't forget to bank the campfire before you go to sleep.
If you bank the 8-ball, it will go into that far pocket.
When we focus on the differences, it is called a heteronym.

(3) A homophone [from Greek *homo-*, same, and *–phoné*, sound] is a word sounding the same as another, but having a different meaning or derivation or spelling.

all   awl
All I know about an awl is that it is a pointed tool.

fair   fare
Do you have enough bus fare to get to the fair?

to/two/too
The two of us want to go with you, too.

QUICK QUIZ
10. to tear up by the roots

(A) debilitate (B) deracinate (C) disperse (D) decaudate

---

there/they're/their

They're trying to tell you that their house is over there.

When we focus on the differences, it is called a heterophone.

Homonym is often considered a broader term that encompasses both homographs and homophones.

Summary: homographs look the same, homophones sound the same, and homonyms look and sound the same.

Q. Is there any difference between *wary* and *leery*?

A. There's no significant difference. Both of them mean cautious —implying a holding back until all evidence has been examined— and both are usually followed by the word *of* : *wary of her advice; leery of her advice*. This is a subjective interpretation, but I always felt that a leery attitude was more cynical or permanent than a wary attitude, which I took to be sensibly cautious. To be honest, though, the dictionary doesn't directly support that interpretation. By the way, another synonym for such caution is *chary*, but it's considered a bit old-fashioned.

Q. I keep hearing people who ought to know better saying, "Between you and I...." Can you help stamp this out?

A. Me will certainly try. Pronouns cause problems because they retain multiple spellings (subject = *I*, object = *me*, possessive = *my* or *mine*). To choose the proper pronoun, you must know what it is doing in its sentence grammatically. *Between* is a preposition, so it requires an object. *You* serves both as subject spelling **and** object spelling, so it causes no problems in this case. But *me* is the spelling needed for an object, so the phrase must read, "*between you and me....*"

Here's the test: when two or more pronouns are involved, test each one <u>separately</u>: *between you* is fine; *between I* obviously is not.

Q. A recent article on obesity in school children called a staff member at a hospital in Scotland an auxologist. What on earth is that?

A. An auxologist is an expert on growth. He or she will study height, weight, organ development, etc., in light of age or stage of development. I suspect that this may be a term used more in Europe than in this country. At any rate, it comes from a Greek word meaning to increase.

Q. Whenever there's a serious problem on my job, a designer with whom I work always remarks, "This doesn't bode well." It seems to mean things aren't going right. Am I correct? He's a bit of a jerk, so I don't want to ask him directly and appear ignorant.

A. You are correct in your surmise. The word *bode* is now considered a bit archaic. That's no surprise, since it goes all the way back to Old Norse, where it meant a messenger. If something doesn't bode well, it's carrying a negative message.

Q. When I was in school many decades ago, teachers drew a strict distinction between *disinterested* and *uninterested*. Now, the words seem to have lost their clarity. What a shame.

A. No argument from me; I must have had the same teachers. *Disinterested* means neutral, dispassionate, and un-

---

Answer 10: (B) deracinate
[L. *de*, away from, + *radix*, root]

When the dandelions cropped up in the yard, he
mercilessly deracinated them.

---

biased. A good referee is disinterested—he calls 'em as he sees 'em. Uninterested means that I'm yawning in boredom—I'm not personally concerned or interested at all.

However, before you and I were even born, the two words had completely opposite meanings. Somewhere in history, they did a flip-flop. So I suppose it's no wonder that there's confusion. I think it's worth preserving the distinction above, however. We'll exempt anyone over 200 years old.

Q. I've seen the term *to blue-pencil* used in reference to editing a manuscript. Does this refer to the actual color used for corrections?

A. It's actually that simple. Editors in the 19th century emended manuscripts with an easy-to-spot blue shade of pencil. These days, if a book manuscript passes through several hands, each participant is assigned a different color to insure accountability.

(An aside: as a young teacher, I used to favor the traditional red pen for making corrections. Then one day an offended student asked me to stop bleeding all over his essays, and I switched to green ink, a much more soothing color.)

Q. What's the difference between a hyphen and a dash?

A. The first difference is size: a dash is longer than a hyphen. In fact, on old typewriters, a double hyphen served as a dash (--).

The second difference is usage. **Hyphens** are commonly used to join compound words (mother-in-law), to join a prefix to a base word (anti-American), and to split a word at the end of a line when there is no room to type it all.

Dashes come in two sizes. The *en-dash*, the shorter of the two, is used, among other things, to separate dates (1945 –

1950). The *em-dash* takes the place of a parenthesis, as in "My father—who believed in personal responsibility—worked hard all his life."

Q. I caught this in the sports section: "She has a veracious and ferocious appetite for the ball," he said. "Nobody gets 20 rebounds a game anymore."

A. Truly, that's a mistake. An appetite may be voracious—ravenous or insatiable. Veracious means honest, truthful, and accurate.

Q. In stories or plays, who's the good guy—the antagonist or the protagonist?

A. The Greeks called the leading actor in a drama (the hero or heroine) the protagonist, from *proto-*, meaning the first or main character. The antagonist was opposed to the main character, from the Greek *ant-*, meaning against. In both cases, the *agon-* word part meant to struggle or contest; it is related to our words *agony* and *agonize*.

Q. When you're trying to focus on something, do you *home in* on it or *hone in* on it? I think I've seen both.

A. *Home in* is correct when you mean to proceed toward a target; think of a homing pigeon. *Hone in* does occur,

---

QUICK QUIZ
11. nuchal: relating to the

(A) palm of the hand   (B) sole of the foot
(C) nape of the neck   (D) cheek

but it is still considered a mistake. Save the word *hone* to mean to sharpen or perfect: *you must hone your skills.*

While I don't wish to make excuses for ignorance, the two words *do* sound alike. It's the same phenomenon that causes some people to write *a tough road to hoe* instead of the proper *tough row to hoe.* The lesson is, you can't always trust your ear. And of course it's all complicated by the phrase *to horn in,* meaning to stick your nose in someone else's business. Ah, hone sweet hone.

Q. Sometimes you'll see a sentence with two parts, where the second part reverses the first part. I'm thinking of John F. Kennedy's, "Ask not what your country can do for you, but what you can do for your country." Is there a name for this figure of speech?

A. This is called chiasmus, and it's named after the Greek equivalent of our letter X, the *chi.* You can see how that criss-cross letter stands as a symbol of reversal. Actually, it's a relatively common way of dressing up an idea. Consider these familiar examples: *When the going gets tough, the tough get going. Eat what you like, and like what you eat. It's not the men in my life, it's the life in my men. Say what you mean and mean what you say. Don't sweat the petty things and don't pet the sweaty things.* Symmetry rules.

Q. Which is correct: *an historic event* or *a historic event?*

A. If you're American, the answer is *a historic event.* The rule determining the choice of *a* or *an* is this: go by what you hear, not by what you see. In other words, if the letter *-h* is sounded out, place *a* in front of it. Test it out: say the word *historic* all by itself. Notice that you say *historic* with a hard *-h,* not *istoric.* So it's *an honest answer, an hourly report, a historic event,* and *a horrible accident.*

Q. Where did we get the expression, *"That's for the birds"*? Why birds instead of some other creature, and what are they getting?

A. There is general agreement that this way of saying that something is worthless or objectionable harks back to the days of horses as the primary mode of transportation. Horses would leave little gifts splattered on the road as they trotted along, and there were undigested oats in them, something that would attract birds. So what at first appears to be a quaint little saying is actually more scatological than it would seem.

Q. I know I've come across a long word which means fear of the number 13, but I can't recall it—let alone spell it!

A. This fear, which may have its origin in the observation that 13 people dined at the Last Supper, is known as triskaidekaphobia. The belief that the number 13 represents danger has even prompted some hotels to avoid designating a 13th floor, instead leaping impossibly from the 12th floor to the 14th. And many people get unduly nervous when Friday the 13th shows up on the calendar. When we examine its parts (based on Greek), we discover that *tris* means three, *kai* means and, *deka* means ten, and *phobia* means fear or irrational response. By the way, though this is the most common spelling of the word, expect to see variations.

Answer 11: (C) nape of the neck
[Arabic *nuha*, spinal cord]

Nuchal tentacles—threadlike organs that protrude from the neck—are found in certain caterpillars.

Q.   Solicit and elicit: are they synonyms?

A.   You'll see them used that way, but they are not identical. When you solicit, you ask for something. When you elicit, you receive something. *The newspaper solicited romantic personal stories for Valentine's Day. The request elicited hundreds of responses.*

Q. On one of your programs, you used the expression "wet your whistle." Shouldn't that have been "whet your whistle"?

A.   No, I'll still drink to "wet your whistle." In her *Dictionary of Clichés*, Christine Ammer endorses it as meaning to have a drink. She remarks that the term has been around at least since Chaucer's *Canterbury Tales*, and gives an example from *The Reeve's Tale* (14th century).

Perhaps you were thinking of the phrase *whet your appetite*, which means to sharpen or increase your appetite. Sometimes, during cocktail hour, we wet our whistle to whet our appetite.

Q.   Usually, verbs are pretty easy. You'll find *was* for the singular and *were* for the plural. However, sometimes you'll see *were* used as a first-person singular, or sometimes the third person, too. For example, "If I were in his shoes, I'd ask for a raise," or "She acts as if she were the Queen of England." Is there any justification for this?

A.   Verb forms used to be much more complicated. You're running into some leftover unsimplified forms that can cause confusion. But let me correct one statement: "You'll find *was* for the singular and *were* for the plural." In fact, the second person singular for the past tense of the verb *to be* is you *were*.

That out of the way, the spelling of a verb deliberately reveals the attitude of a speaker or writer. We call this the mood or mode of a verb, and there are three possibilities: the indicative, the imperative, and the subjunctive.

(1) If the writer makes a statement of real or supposed fact, expresses an opinion, or asks a question, she is using the indicative mood and will choose certain verb spellings. *She was here. That is true. Am I in your way? Nominations are now closed.* This is the most common form of a verb.

(2) If the writer issues a request or a command, or gives directions, he is using the imperative mood. *Turn off the lights. Please scratch my back. Turn north at the gas station. Go away!* In this mood, the subject is always "you" (the person addressed) and it doesn't even get written or said.

(3) The last set of spellings and pairings is called the subjunctive mood, and it is an endangered species. Even as we speak, many of its traditional forms are being dropped in favor of indicative mood forms. Here are the remnants. Sophisticated (or stubborn) writers use the subjunctive mood for

  a. Conditions contrary to fact.
      If I were President.... (I'm not.)
      If it were not snowing... (It is snowing.)
  b. Wishes or desires.
      I wish I were taller. Thy will be done.
  c. Suppositions.
      Suppose he were to ask you to marry him.
      Were I to attend the wedding, would I be welcome?
  d. Concessions.
      Though that be true, we must do the right thing.
  e. Improbable condition.
      He worked as if he were living the last 60 seconds of his life.
  f. <u>That clauses</u> expressing parliamentary motions, resolutions, demands, necessity, recommendations, or requests.
      I move that the proposal be shelved.

I insist that he go see a doctor.
We recommend that she be fired.
It is necessary that I be excused.

The fact is that many people will write their way around the subjunctive mood. *If I attend, will I be welcome? Even if that's true, we must do the right thing. I move that we shelve the proposal. I must be excused.* Be that as it may, and would that it were easier, traces of the subjunctive still remain.

Q.   How serious a mistake is it to end a sentence with a preposition?

A.   This is one of the persistent grammatical myths of modern times, along with the "rule" that you're not supposed to split an infinitive (<u>to</u> boldly <u>go</u>). I'm sure your teachers told you it was wrong; so did mine. But they overstated the case because that's how *they* had been taught, and their teachers before them. *Fowler's Modern English Usage*, 3rd edition, thinks it may have become fixed in popular opinion by John Dryden, 17th century British poet, dramatist, and critic.

The reason this "rule" doesn't fit the English language is that it was derived from grammar books discussing the **Latin** language. For clarity in Latin, the preposition had to come before its object. And you *can't* split an infinitive in Latin because that verb form always exists as one inseparable word. In English, it's always two words or more, with the preposition *to* being at least implied. Take the Star Trek phrase in English, *to boldly go where no one has gone before*. In Latin, it's *ire audacter*. There's no way to split the infinitive (*ire*) unless you were to do something weird, such as *i- [audacter] -re*, which no respectable toga-wearing Roman would do.

Here's a good way to survive conflicting opinions: as long as the sentence is not awkward or unclear, don't waste a lot of time worrying about split infinitives or sentence-ending prepositions.

Let Winston Churchill, no slouch at the English language, have the last word. Allegedly, Sir Winston was editing a proof of one of his books when he noticed that an editor had clumsily rearranged one of his sentences so that it wouldn't end with a preposition. Churchill scribbled in the margin, "This is the sort of bloody nonsense up with which I will not put." He was joking.

Q. There seems to be a disturbing trend toward phrasing ideas in a negative way. For instance, a magazine article contained this: "For a not inconsiderable sum, the company will go through your closets and bring your wardrobe up to date." And a politician in Lansing recently was quoted as saying, "I am not unaware of the plight of the homeless."

A. It has not escaped my attention. My assessment is that it's a way of evading direct statements, which many politicians and public figures seem to think are traps instead of opportunities. It's also a way of padding ideas; the advantage to a politician is that he holds the microphone just a little bit longer. But when it's not overused, it's a legitimate figure of speech known as litotes.

Generally, it's better to frame statements in a positive way unless something is being denied or contradicted. Thus, write *for a hefty price* instead of *for a not inconsiderable sum; I know about* rather than *I am not ignorant of; I*

Answer 12: (A) hostile
[L. *inimicus*, enemy]

He spoke to us in a cold, inimical tone of voice.

---

noticed rather than *I am not unaware of*. Not without reason are you encouraged to write non-negative statements.

Q. Where did the axiom, "Don't buy a pig in a poke" come from?

A. First of all, a poke is a bag or a pouch. Allegedly, it was a common scam at medieval marketplaces to put a dead cat in a sack [*shades of Dr. Seuss!*] and pass it off as a suckling pig, a relatively expensive delicacy. The scam artist would manage to get away before the rube opened the bag and discovered the ruse. One of the first written instances occurs way back in the 14th century, and to this day, the saying still means, "Don't buy something sight unseen."
Connected to this saying is "to let the cat out of the bag." By the way, our word *pocket* comes from the same source as *poke*.

Q. I'm getting very tired of hearing *nuclear* pronounced as noo-kyoo-lur. Why can't people get it right?

A. The power of habit and of regional pronunciation, I suppose. Two more frequently abused words are real-uh-tor (realtor) and ath-uh-leet (athlete). Notice that in all three cases, the extra syllable (*uh*, the schwa sound) comes between two consonants. When your mouth glides from consonant to consonant—or even when you say the name of a consonant slowly—there's often a latent *uh* sound buried in there. As my mother used to say of many things, it's not an excuse, but it is an explanation.

☞   BUMPER STICKER   ☜
My wife really likes to make pottery,
but to me it's just kiln time

Q. What happened to the distinction between *shall* and *will*?

A. You must have been in school a long time ago; this is an 18th century prescription that has fallen by the wayside. The old rule had two parts:
1. To indicate simple futurity, use *shall* in the first person (I, we) and *will* in the second and third person (you, he,she, it, they).
2. To show determination (I *will* go!) use *will* in the first person and *shall* in the second and third person.

The word *shall* has practically disappeared except in legal documents. In everyday use, one of the few times it comes up is when we politely, and somewhat archly, ask permission to do something—*Shall I turn out the lights?* There's nothing wrong with observing the old distinctions, but if your audience doesn't know about them, all that subtlety will go to waste.

Q. What is a Michigan Bankroll?

A. It's a term involved in scams. A number of dollar bills are wadded or rolled together with a $100 bill on the outside to give the appearance of a large bankroll. [1914, *Variety*] It's also called a Philadelphia Bankroll or an Oklahoma Bankroll. And then there's a Chicago Bankroll, which you throw on the ground if you're being mugged in order to let you run away.

QUICK QUIZ
13. fractious

(A) damaged (B) unruly (C) delicious (D) nervous

Lest you think that only these places have been maligned, here are a few more items involving cities or states.

- Alaska Tennis Shoes: knee-high rubber boots
- Arkansas Lizards: lice
- Arkansas Toothpick: hunting knife used for fighting
- California Bible: deck of cards
  (Also called *California prayer book*)
- California Blankets: newspapers used to sleep on and under
- California Cornflakes: cocaine
- Chicago Overcoat: a coffin
- Chicago Pineapple: hand grenade
- Chicago Voter: dead person who votes early and often
- Florida Snow: cocaine
- Green Bay fly: the mayfly
- Jersey Barrier: concrete slab used to keep vehicles from crossing a median
- Jersey Lightning: gin or inferior whiskey
- Kentucky Breakfast: bourbon
- Kentucky Fried: alcohol intoxicated
- Milwaukee Goiter: large gut caused by excessive beer drinking
- Nantucket sleigh ride: fast towing of a whaling boat by a harpooned whale
- Nebraska Sign: indication of death, when the line on an EEG is as flat as the state of Nebraska
- Nevada Nickel: a $5 chip
- New York Minute: extremely short period of time
- Philadelphia Decision: boxing judges vote for the hometown favorite
- Philadelphia Lawyer: shrewd attorney adept at the discovery and manipulation of legal technicalities

Q. Can *adjacent* and *adjoining* be swapped?

A. Many people do, but I'd suggest keeping them separate. Adjacent primarily means close to or lying near, but not actually touching. *My house and my brother's house are adjacent.* Adjoining implies that items are so close that they're contiguous—they're touching. *The door to the adjoining suite was locked.*

Q. People are getting pretty sloppy about acronyms. I saw a bank ad that spoke of its convenient ATM machine.

A. I assume you're referring to the redundancy involved in Automated Teller Machine machine. My guess is that some folks have no idea what the initials stand for. We see the same thing happening with PIN number (Personal Identification Number), UPC code (Universal Product Code), HIV virus (Human Immunodeficiency Virus), SAT test (Scholastic Aptitude Test), and the CPI index (Consumer Price Index).

By the way, an acronym can be pronounced as if it were a word (NATO). The examples above, except for PIN, are initialisms.

☞ ALSO KNOWN AS ☜
Strike: To take down a sail or
stage set

Answer 13: (B) unruly
[L. *refringere*, to break off]

The prisoner was fractious and uncooperative.

Q. I was told that the phrase "dead ringer" started because in the 19th century, people who worried about being buried alive used to order coffins equipped with a device that would ring a bell over their grave if they woke up six feet under. If this is true, it's about as gruesome a phrase as I can imagine.

A. In the days before embalming, there is evidence that people were occasionally buried alive and that entrepeneurs did sell such devices. But death has nothing to do with "dead ringer." Instead, that phrase comes from horse racing, and means an exact double. A ringer is a horse substituted for another horse to defraud the bookies by messing with the odds. The word dead as used here means exact, as in the phrases *in a dead heat* or *dead on target*. The "ringer" part goes back to *ringing the changes*, a competitive sport among church bell ringers, believe it or not, in which they try all the possible combinations on a set of bells without repeating a peal. A ringer would be close to, but not exactly like, the original combination.

Q. Could you comment on some of the strange marks that occur in foreign words?

A. They are known as diacritical marks, and they help with pronunciation. Here are a few: (1) The acute accent shows a rising inflection (résumé); (2) The cedilla shows that a -c should be pronounced as -s (façade); (3) The circumflex appears in some French words (fête); (4) The diaeresis—umlaut in German—shows that a vowel is pronounced separately (Chloë); (5) The grave accent indicates that a final syllable should be pronounced separately (blessèd); (6) The tilde shows that a Spanish -n should be pronounced -ny (señorita).

Q. Ambiguous and ambivalent: don't they mean the same thing?

A. Not in their primary meanings. Something *ambiguous* is open to more than one interpretation (an ambiguous response), while *ambivalent* usually applies to contradictory feelings—a love/hate relationship, for example. Perhaps you're thinking of their secondary meanings, in which *ambiguous* can mean uncertain because of double meaning and *ambivalent* can mean uncertain as to which course to follow. To differentiate them, think of *ambiguous* as a mental state and *ambivalent* as an emotional state.

Q. What can you tell me about the suffix *-bad* which occurs in many town names in the Mideast, such as Islamabad?

A. You're right about its frequency. A quick search turned up Ahmedabad, Ashgabad, Ashkhabad, Hyderabad, Moradabad, Secunderabad, and Jalalabad. The suffix *-abad* comes from a Persian word meaning a settlement or village. It is akin to the *-ville* ending in many American town names, such as Stevensville.

☞ ALSO KNOWN AS ☜
skein: group of geese flying in formation

QUICK QUIZ
14. an impressive array

(A) panache (B) panolia (C) panegyric (D) panoply

Q.   I heard you use the terms denotation and connotation on your program, but I didn't catch their meanings.

A.   Denotation may be called the dictionary definition of a word, its stark and literal meaning. The connotation of the same word involves the whole set of associations—rational and emotional—which you have attached to it by experience. The denotation of a word is objective; its connotation is personal. The word *snake* is a good example. Everyone looking it up in the same dictionary will derive the same meaning. But some people find snakes attractive and fascinating and become herpetologists. Others can't get past a deeply primitive fear and become herpetophobes.

Q.   When I was a youngster (many years ago!), people used the phrase *spick and span* to describe something which was clean and shiny. If it weren't for the cleaning products which bear that brand name, I suspect that it would now be archaic.

A.   You're right; I don't hear that expression much anymore, either. In fact, the two words that compose it are definitely obsolete. A spick was a spike or nail, and a span was a wood chip. In the days of sailing ships, a new ship was described as spick and span because every single nail and every piece of wood was new. One of the earliest written uses of the term makes it clear that spick and span meant new: "They were all in goodly gilt armours, and brave purple cassocks upon them, spicke, and spanne newe." [Thomas North's 1579 translation of Plutarch's *Lives*]

Q. I see a lot of computer companies which spell their name with a capital letter halfway through the word, such as PostScript or EasyWriter or NeXT. What gives?

A. *The Jargon Dictionary* refers to this as BiCapitalization. I'm sure companies follow this practice to make their brand name stand out from the others, but it wears thin after a while. I've also seen it called intercaps.

Q. Why is spelling such a mess in our language?

A. Ah, you noticed. It's a matter of history. Just at the time that our language was moving away from its Germanic roots and developing into Middle English, the Normans took over Britain and made French the official language. For quite a while, lowly English was the language of the peasant class, and they didn't learn it in school. Spelling was a matter of great indifference, further complicated by French doublets. In the 14th and 15th centuries, there was a massive shift in pronunciation; try reading Chaucer in the original and you'll see what I mean. And then, just as spelling would have become simplified to match the changed pronunciation, along came William Caxton with the newfangled printing press. With mass production, a standard version of English with standard spelling became a consideration and a battleground for the next two centuries. Caxton used a lot of soon-to-be outmoded spellings, thus freezing them in place. And that's why we have so many words with letters that we no longer pro-

---

Answer 14: (D) panoply
[Gr. *hopla*, armor]

A panoply of colorful flags adorned the roof of the stadium.

---

nounce. Over the centuries, many people have tried to simplify spelling, but to little avail.

Q. How do I know when to use *who, which* and *that*?

A. *Who* refers to people, *which* refers to things, and *that* refers to either. A further rule has to do with restrictive clauses (essential information) and nonrestrictive clauses (optional information). For a restrictive clause, use **that**: *The snow that fell last night delayed the school bus.* For a nonrestrictive clause, use **which**: *The snow, which was about a foot deep, delayed the school bus.* Generally speaking, if the clause is not set off by commas, use the word *that*. The answer that I just gave will get you through many problems. My answer, which works in most cases, will get you through many problems.

Q. I'm told that my doctor will palpate me during my next visit. Will that hurt?

A. Not unless she has cold fingers. It means to examine or explore a part of the body by touch. Related words are palpable and palpitation. (Say, if you write a story on your hand, would that be that Palp Fiction?)

Bulletin:
A truck loaded with thousands of copies of Roget's Thesaurus crashed as it left a New York publishing house yesterday, according to the Associated Press. Witnesses were stunned, startled, aghast, taken aback, stupefied, confused, punchy, shocked, rattled, paralyzed, dazed, bewildered, mixed up, surprised, awed, dumbfounded, nonplused, flabbergasted, astounded, amazed, confounded, astonished, boggled, overwhelmed, horrified, numbed, and perplexed.

Q. Even though the word *tax* has only three letters, it has the impact of a four-letter word. Where did it come from?

A. From a movie entitled, "The Attax of the IRS Pod People." Serious up. There was an Old French word *taxer*, which meant to tax, so it's not a recent burden to humankind. Ultimately, it goes back to the Latin word *tangere*, which meant to touch. The image that pops into my head is of a toga-wearing tax gatherer sliding coins across a counting table to make sure that the price is right. A touching scene. Other words formed from the popular *tang/tact* root include contact, tangent, intact, tangible, and tactile.

Q. What is meant by dangling participles?

A. First, a participle is a verb that has been converted to an adjective. Therefore, like all adjectives, it needs to be closely connected to a noun or a noun substitute. We say that a participle dangles when we mean that it doesn't clearly point to the word it modifies. Here's an example: *While riding my bicycle down the alley, a cat ran in front of me.* Sounds like the cat was on the bicycle, which is ridiculous. The correction involves nailing the participial phrase to the word it modifies: *While I was riding my bicycle down the alley, a cat ran in front of me.* Another example: *Spattered with paint, my mother cleaned the window pane.* We can't tell who was spattered with paint—your mother or the window. Try this instead: *My mother cleaned the paint-spattered window pane.* Practice on this one: *Peering out the windows on the northwest side of the Traverse Area District Library, a blanket of white snow covers the ground.*

Q.   It drives me crazy when I hear people say duck tape. It's DUCT tape.

A.   Now don't quack up on us. You're correct, of course; it was originally designed to seal heating and air-conditioning ducts. It's another case of spelling what we hear. Many people don't give a strong pronunciation to that final -*t* when they say the word. But if you'll stop by your local hardware store, you'll notice that one company has chosen to call its product Duck Tape. Sticky business, this.

Q.   Did you ever notice how many common phrases come in pairs? I mean, there's now and again, to and fro, cut and dried, here and there, and so on. Why is that?

A.   It seems that symmetrical phrases are more appealing to the ear. Notice that most of them are cliches, too: bag and baggage, bricks and mortar, far and away, hot and bothered, thick and thin, fast and furious, wild and woolly, lock and load. Because they are rhythmical and pleasant to hear, they get overused. Now it's time to cut and run before I'm left high and dry.

Q.   Where did the admonition to *mind your p's and q's* come from?

A.   No one knows for sure, but that doesn't stop people from arguing vociferously about the origin. Here are some of the explanations that are usually brought forward.

1. It's advice to a child learning its letters to be careful not to mix up the handwritten lower-case letters *p* and *q*.
2. It's advice to a printer's apprentice, for whom the backward-facing metal type letters would be especially confusing.

3. It's advice to a barman not to confuse the letters *p* and *q* (pints and quarts) on the account tally for drinks consumed by the patrons.
4. It's an abbreviation of *mind your please's and thank you's*.
5. It's an instruction from a French dancing master to be sure to perform the dance figures *pieds* and *queues* accurately.
6. It's a warning to 19th century sailors not to soil their navy pea-jackets (p's) with their tarred *queues*, that is, their pigtails.

For what it's worth, the second one seems most likely to me, given that setting type in the old days was done with the individual letters upside down and backwards on the table. But then, why isn't it also *mind your b's and d's*?

Q.   I collected stamps as a girl, and in those days, a *cachet* was a commemorative envelope used to mark an anniversary or special event. So when I came across this in a magazine, I was puzzled: "Federal courts have a certain cachet which state courts lack."

A.   Cachet has several meanings, and one of them is "a quality or mark of distinction." It comes from the French *cacher*, to press—an imprinting—and farther back, from a Latin term meaning to force or pack together.

Incidentally, the word *cache* (pronounced kash) comes from the same source, though it means a hiding place.

Answer 15: (C) expurgate
[L. *purgare*, to purify]

Thomas Bowdler published an expurgated version of Shakespeare in 1818.

Q.   My son's English book keeps using the term inflection. Explain, please.

A.   An inflection is a change in the form of a word. In nouns, the basic shift is from singular to plural, and we signal that by a change in spelling: *van* becomes *vans*, *woman* becomes *women*, and *alumnus* becomes *alumni*. In verbs, there are even more changes. Thus, *speak* changes to *speaks*, *spoke*, *spoken*, and *speaking*, depending on the number, person, mood, or time. You're lucky that your son's book didn't use the buzzword *paradigm*, which is a synonym.

Q.   Is there a difference between *authoritative* and *authoritarian*?

A.   Yes, there is, and it's an important distinction, since one is a compliment and the other is an insult. Authoritative means expert, speaking with recognized authority: *She wrote the authoritative book on prison reform.* Authoritarian, on the other hand, means favoring complete obedience or subjection to authority, as opposed to individual freedom: *In spite of his promises, he turned out to be an authoritarian leader who oppressed his own people.*

Q.   Is there a Greek or Latin word part which means deep? I'm trying to come up with a classy word for *deep thinker*.

A.   Do not try this at home, folks. I'm normally the enemy of obfuscatory words, but I'll override my conscience and help anyway.

Bathy- is a standard word part meaning deep, and of the many word parts referring to thought or judgment, *-gnos-* seems to work well, since it refers to ideas accessible only to a few. So bathygnostic seems to be a suitable neologism for a deep thinker. By the way, there already exists the word bathysophical, which means relating to a knowledge of the depths of the sea or of the things found there.

Q. Is there much of a difference between an illusion and a delusion?

A. Actually, there is. An illusion is something that deceives by producing a false or misleading impression of reality that can be corrected: *The puddle on the road turned out to be an optical illusion.* A delusion is a false belief or opinion resistant to reason or confrontation with fact: *He suffered from delusions of grandeur.*

Don't confuse allusion with illusion. An allusion is a passing or casual reference, an incidental mention of something: *She made an allusion to her father's illness.*

Q. I've got one for you: what does a baby changing station change them into?

A. Funny. It reminds me of a tool I saw advertised on TV the other day—a hand chopper, they call it. Gruesome! And the Discovery Channel had this: "Clint Burrows is a dangerous wild animal consultant." Don't turn your back on him.

☞ BUMPER STICKER ☜
When you dream in color, it's a pigment of your imagination

QUICK QUIZ
16. punctilious

(A) attentive (B) wounded (C) hasty (D) morbid

Q. I know that "all the world is my oyster" means bountiful opportunities are available to me, but why an oyster?

A. Probably because you can get a pearl by prying open an oyster. Shakespeare used the saying in *The Merry Wives of Windsor* when he had the character Pistol say, "Why, then, the world's mine oyster which I with sword will open."

Q. Today is Lewis Carroll's birthday, and in his honor I remind you that he invented doublets.

In doublets, or ladder, you transform one word into another by changing a single letter in each step, so that each link in the chain is a valid word. For example, to change MORE into LESS with 3 links: MORE, lore, lose, loss, LESS

A. Thanks for the reminder. Here are some more.

- Make DOOR†LOCK†(3 links): DOOR , boor , book, look, LOCK
- Put MILK into PAIL (3 links): MILK, mill, pill, pall, PAIL
- From RIP to SEW (3 links): RIP, rap, sap, saw, SEW
- From MICE to RATS (3 links): MICE, mite, mate, mats, RATS

Q. I saw a traffic sign that urged me to "Go Slow." Shouldn't that have been slowly?

A. Present-day custom tends to favor slowly in formal writing, but slow is also correct. Slow is one of those native adverbs that once had the same form for adverb and adjective. A few others in that class are *hard, fast,* and *late.* He worked hard, not hardly. She drove fast, not fastly. They worked late, not lately. In spoken or casual use, "Go slow" is not offensive.

Q. Is there any difference between repressing and suppressing thoughts or feelings?

A. Common practice seems to hinge on whether the exclusion is conscious or unconscious. Thus, to suppress is to *deliberately* exclude thoughts or feelings or their expression. To repress is to *automatically* exclude painful impulses, desires, or fears; you don't even realize you are doing it. In contexts outside of psychology, both mean *to put down by force, quell, subdue.*

Q. Where did "not worth a tinker's damn" come from?

A. It means worthless. Especially in Scotland and Ireland, a tinker was a traveling mender of household utensils, an itinerant. A swear word coming from him was especially worthless, since there were so many. The Victorians tried to clean it up later by claiming that a dam was the plug he used in soldering tin plates, but that's really an afterthought.

☞ THE GAME OF THE NAME ☜
Bradley comes from the Old English broad clearing

Answer 16: (A) attentive
[L. *punctum*, point]

The young man was so punctilious that we
thought he'd never finish mopping the floor.

Q. Whatever happened to semicolons? I just don't see many any more.

A. Writing styles change, and in our day, the style is to write short, punchy sentences; hence, semicolons aren't needed as much as in the days of long sentences. It's still a good idea to use them for variety.

Warning: don't think of semicolons as some kind of strong comma; you'll misuse them if you do. Rather, think of a semicolon as another kind of period. If you see a period between two sentences that are closely connected because of content, rhythm, cause and effect, etc., you may replace the period with a semicolon. *My brother is an accountant; my sister is a lawyer.*

Q. Talk about back formation. I came across the word treeware in a computer magazine to describe an old-fashioned paper, rather than software, manual of instructions.

A. Actually, that's sort of catchy. Let me share a couple that I came across. Phonesia has been defined as the affliction of dialing a phone number and forgetting the person you were calling just as she answers. I can relate to that. The other word is Fauxriental—orientally-themed furniture sold at large furniture retailers such as Furniture Depot, often displaying Chinese/Japanese characters inappropriately (e.g. upside down).

☞   WORD FACT   ☜

Though they seem unconnected, the following words all descended from the Indo-European root steig- (to stick or pointed): stitch, etiquette, ticket, extinguish, tiger, steak, and thistle.

Q. I work for a bill collecting agency, and I keep running across *discrete* being mistaken for *discreet* in some of our internal memos.

A. Hey, I paid that bill! And the check is in the mail. You're right, of course; the spelling of those two is dangerously close. Discreet means showing prudence and circumspection. Discrete means separate, or consisting of unconnected, distinct parts. *The corporation has three discrete divisions, and the managers are very discreet when it comes to company secrets.*

Q. How do you know whether to double a consonant at the end of a word when adding a suffix? My son is entering a spelling bee and this would help.

A. There is a three-step process that will help when you add a suffix to a word that ends in a single consonant. You must answer all three questions:

(1) YES or NO: does the suffix begin with a vowel?
  Examples: -er, -ing YES; -ful, -ment NO

(2) YES or NO: are the last 3 letters of the original word a consonant-vowel-consonant (in that exact order)?
  Examples: win, forget YES; greet, treat NO

(3) YES or NO: does the accent of the original word fall on the last syllable? (One-syllable words get an automatic YES answer).
  Examples: stop, begin YES; secret, benefit NO

QUICK QUIZ
17. the rod on a sundial that shows the time:

(A) gnomon (B) jess (C) frass (D) aglet

If you get a YES answer to *all three* of these questions, **double** the final consonant of the word before adding the suffix. *(forgettable, winning)*

If you get a NO answer to *any* of these questions, do not double the final consonant before adding a suffix. *(forgetful, greeting)*

Q.   Log on to the internet if you want some unintended laughs. One web site talks about what it calls "a hare-raising threat" from ghosts in the guy's house.

A.   No doubt a ghost named Bunny. There used to be a tongue-in-check statistical theory that if you sat one million monkeys in front of typewriters, eventually they would reproduce Shakespeare's plays. The internet has soundly disproved that. The spelling should be hair-raising, of course. It refers to the raised bumps on the skin that cause hairs to rise. The technical term is horripilation.

Q.   In a title, which words get capitalized?

A.   Capitalize the first letter of each word of a title, except for minor words such as prepositions, articles, and coordinating conjunctions. However, even these minor words are capitalized when they are the first or the last word of your title: *The Origin of Consciousness in the Breakdown of the Bicameral Mind.*

Q.   Someone was described as a coniologist in an article about volcanoes. Is that a fancy term for a volcano expert?

A.   Not directly. A coniologist is an expert on atmospheric dust, so you can see the connection. A vulcanologist is the volcano expert. I'm always amazed at some of the titles that experts bear. There are pterylologists (feathers), pogonologists (beards), typhlologists (blindness), nosologists (diseases), and zymologists (fermentation). I suppose they have to study all those years just to learn how to pronounce their specialties.

Q. A lot of cop shows on TV use the term M.O. What does that stand for?

A. Modus operandi—a method of functioning. It serves to illustrate the fact that a number of Latin words and phrases were swallowed whole by the English language. There's *caveat* (let him beware), a fancy word for a warning. It also shows up in the phrase *caveat emptor*, let the buyer beware. *Habeas corpus* means you may have the body, *alma mater* means nurturing mother, and *persona non grata* means an unwelcome person. *Tempus fugit* (time flies), so *carpe diem* (seize the day). This could go on *ad infinitum*.

Q. We frequently use the phrase *hard of hearing*, so why isn't there a *hard of seeing*?

A. You're not going to believe this, but there *is* a hard of seeing. Here's a quote from New York State Services for the Blind: " Sometimes people refer to low vision as being 'hard of seeing' or a little bit blind." Stranger yet, here's some dialogue from the *Smelly Car* episode of Seinfeld:

Answer 17: (A) gnomon
[Gr. *gnomon*, interpreter]

If the gnomon is bent or deformed, the sundial will be inaccurate.

Jerry: "Do you smell something?"

Elaine: "Do I smell something? What am I, hard of smelling?"

And to top things off, a quote from the Times Picayunne: "Sometimes, there's just too much of a good thing, especially when flavors are boosted to levels that seem pitched to the hard-of-tasting."

Examples of *hard of touching* elude me. Any evidence out there?

Q.   Why are ministers called Pastor?

A.   *Pastor* is a Latin word meaning shepherd, and it is a reflection of John 10:11 (*I am the Good Shepherd*) and of John 21: 15-16 (*Feed my lambs....Feed my sheep*).

Q.   What is a pigeon language?

A.   Obviously, a language that requires you to bob your head up and down while speaking. Just kidding. This must be something you heard rather than read. It's actually spelled pidgin, and it's a very simplified form of language— often a simplified blend of a couple of existing languages. It's used by groups who don't speak each other's language, but still need to communicate, usually for business purposes. As it develops, it has a very simple grammar and a small, but useful, vocabulary. Think of some of those old jungle movies: "Me kill 'em cheetah." That's a form of pidgin. If a pidgin lasts long enough to become the first language of a group, it is said to be creolized. *Ooops! I just creolized that it's time to feed the pidgins.*

☞   BUMPER STICKER   ☜
Dijon vu - the same mustard as before

Q. My church is going to have a white elephant sale, and while some of us were setting things up, we began to puzzle over the origin of the term.

A. The first mention in writing in English was in 1663, according to the *Oxford English Dictionary*. The image was taken from an old story about a King of Siam. Only he could own a sacred albino elephant, but because it was sacred and couldn't be used for work, it was a burden on him. The story goes on to say that every time the king encountered an obnoxious courtier, he would give him the gift of a white elephant, thus draining the courtier's finances and getting revenge. So a white elephant has come to mean something useless that is just valuable enough not to throw away. Giving it to a worthy fundraiser is a great idea.

Q. Have you noticed that no one dies anymore? They "pass" or "get called to a higher service."

A. Say, I'll take a pass on death if they allow me. There may be more euphemisms about dying than about any other subject. There's an element of fear involved, and some people act as if dying is an indelicate act that one should be ashamed of. I'm with you: bring back death and dying instead of *bought the farm, cashed in their chips, crossed the Great Divide, earned a heavenly promotion, went someplace else, went to greener pastures, jumped the last hurdle, laid down his burden, left the building, met her maker, went home,* or *removed himself from the voting list.*

QUICK QUIZ
18. objurgate:

(A) to support   (B) to scold   (C) to murder   (D) to heal

Q.   *Bemuse* and *amuse*: are they synonyms?

A.   No, they are not. Bemuse means to confuse or bewilder; amuse means to entertain or cause laughter. Of course, it might amuse you to bemuse people.

Q.   I just came across something called *kangaroo words* on Richard Lederer's web site. Are you aware of them?

A.   I have encountered them. A kangaroo word is one that carries within its spelling, in normal order, a smaller word that is a synonym for itself. It uses the analogy of a joey in its mother's pouch. Someone named A. Ackley (web site, *The Teacher's Desk*) claims she invented the game in 1996, and she offers these examples:

Starting Word	Kangaroo Word
slithered	slid
perimeter	rim
indolent	idle
prattle	prate
evacuate	vacate

Try playing with these: encourage, prosecute, calumnies, joviality, curtail.   * (answers on page 80)

Q.   My granddaughter has problems with a lisp; her *-s* sounds like *-th*. Will she outgrow this?

A.   That's a question beyond my expertise. The older she is, the more my instinct is to tell the family to take her to a speech therapist. I have a granddaughter who used to call me gwandpa, and I'm happy to say that she outgrew it. On the other hand, trouble pronouncing letters often perdures into adulthood for cultural reasons. For instance, Chinese speakers characteristically have problems pronouncing the letter -*r*, instead substituting the letter -*l*, as in *velly good flied lice*. It's called lambdacism—named after the Greek letter lambda. But the Japanese characteristically reverse the process and substitute the letter -*r* for -*l*, as in *ret me roose, Engrish rady*. This is called rhotacism, after the Greek letter rho.

Q.   Especially in textbooks, I come across the terms *addenda, corrigenda*, and *errata*. What do they mean?

A.   These are the plural forms of *addendum, corrigendum*, and *erratum*. That should clear things up, no? Addenda are supplements to a text; they usually appear after the last chapter. A list of the errors found in a book after its printing—along with their corrections—is known as corrigenda. Errata are the same as corrigenda; they are inserted into the book before it goes out the factory door. If the book goes into another edition, these corrections are then incorporated into the text.

Q.   Shouldn't there be a distinction between *contagious* and *infectious*? I'm thinking specifically about diseases.

A.   I have no background in medicine, so I'll answer this linguistically. *Contagious* is based on a Latin root that means touch, so a contagious disease implies direct contact with a patient. An *infectious* disease spreads via a microorganism, so direct contact is not necessary. Medical use of the terms may be more precise, so take two aspirin, drink plenty of fluids, and consult your physician. It's interesting that both

---

Answer 18: (B) to scold
[L. *ob*, against + *iurgare*, scold]

All the hypocritical whining and objurgating in the
world will not alter their determination.

---

terms have been extended beyond medical use. We speak of an infectious laugh or a contagious smile, and noxious ideas are sometimes damned with these adjectives.

Q. How old is the English language?

A. I'm not being evasive when I say that it's hard to tell; put it in the vicinity of 1,400 years. The best we can do is point to the first texts written in an earlier form of our language. They date back to the year 700, but certainly the language was spoken before then. Germanic tribes (Angles, Saxons, Jutes) invaded the British Isles in the 5ᵗʰ century, and their dialects provided the foundation for Old English. But when was the magic moment when Germanic turned into a distinct Old English? History is speechless on this point. We do know that we have to approach Old English as a foreign language. It had some letters that no longer exist, no one worried much about capital letters, punctuation and spacing, the word order was much different, and even the sounds were alien. "Our Father who art in heaven" was rendered, "Fæder ure, þu þe eart on heofonum." It's like meeting a relative for the first time and noticing a vague family resemblance.

Q. Help me settle a bet with my sister. I say the difference between a diagnosis and a prognosis is that a diagnosis concerns the present and a prognosis concerns the future. Right?

A. That's a succinct way to summarize it. A diagnosis is the process of identifying the nature and cause of a disease and reaching a conclusion. A prognosis is a prediction of its probable outcome. So you're right. By the way, notice the letter sequence *-gnos-*, a very useful word part. It comes from

* (*Answers from page 78*): urge, sue, lies, joy, cut

the Greek, and it means knowledge. It shows up in agnostic (one who believes we can't know for sure if there's a God), baragnosis (loss of the ability to perceive weight by lifting an object), bibliognostic (one who has a comprehensive knowledge of books), and Gnostics (religious sect that claimed to have secret knowledge of God).

Q. I know that canine is the adjective for a dog and that feline refers to a cat. Does every animal have a similar fancy adjective?

A. I believe so. Let's run through a few, confining the list to those ending in *-ine*.

piscine = fish	cervine = deer
cricetine = gerbil	murine = mouse
leporine = rabbit	sciurine = squirrel
mephitine = skunk	vulpine = fox
ceratorhine = rhinoceros	anatine = duck
anserine = goose	larine = gull

This is just a sampling, of course. One of my favorites is the adjective for parrots, psittacine, because it reminds me of the sputtering sound of a bird completely at a loss for words. Say, if a parrot used only long words, would it be Polly-syllabic?

☞　　　　WORD FACT　　　　☜

Many people treat the word amateur as a negative term—a rookie, a fumbler, an incompetent—but it really means someone who loves what he or she is doing (L. *amare*, to love).

QUICK QUIZ
19. to confirm or manifest:

(A) extenuate　　(B) palliate　　(C) confute　　(D) evince

Q. I believe that both elegies and eulogies are delivered at funerals. So what's the difference?

A. That's not quite correct. A eulogy is a speech of tribute, especially praising someone who has died. It could be given at a funeral. An elegy is a poem (or song) written to mourn a dead person. One of the most famous elegies was Thomas Gray's *Elegy Written in a Country Churchyard*. Other speeches of praise include encomium, panegyric, laudation, homage, accolade, and tribute.

Q. I want to nominate two words for total destruction: event and facility. They are used to inflate phrases, and they drive me crazy.

A. I've noticed an outbreak of their use, too. There are no movies anymore; instead, we have "movie events." Television isn't far behind when it advertises "a television event." And I've heard medical personnel refer to "a heart event." In addition, we run into church facilities, museum facilities, housing facilities, and so on. The folks who lean on such clichés should learn this principle: longer is not always smarter or more significant. Call a spade a spade, not an excavating implement.

Q. A memo from my managing editor warned us reporters to "site our sources" when we write a story. And they carp about *our* mistakes!

A. Fishy, indeed. Cite was the word needed, meaning to reveal the origin of a fact or quote. A site is a location. Perhaps your M.E. should start a web cite.

☞   BUMPER STICKER   ☜
Acupuncture is a jab well done

Q. I have a question in regards to the apostrophe. We are writing the rules for the Farmers Market. When used as a title for something, would we use an apostrophe showing possession in Farmers? I look on it as being a market made up of farmers, not belonging to farmers, hence not using the apostrophe.

A. You bring up an interesting point about apostrophes. Just a few years ago, Farmers' Market would have been the required standard. Now, in many company names or institutional titles, the apostrophe is being deliberately left out, often as a space-saving move. Citizens Bank comes to mind, as do Consumers Energy and Department of Veterans Affairs. So, even though some old-timers may wince when they notice a missing apostrophe, current practice is on your side because of the distinction you mentioned. Apostrophes cause so much trouble that there is now an Apostrophe Protection Society in Great Britain;
see http://www.apostrophe.fsnet.co.uk/

Q. It seems to me that *fortuitous* is being mistaken for *fortunate*. They are not the same and should not be interchanged.

A. You'll hear no argument from me. *Fortuitous* means "happening by accident or chance." Such an accident has no quality attached to it; that is, it could be lucky or unlucky. The word *fortunate* carries the sole meaning of something desirable or good. So there is a real difference between "It

---

Answer 19: (D) evince
[L. *vincere*, to conquer]

She evinced her delight by breaking into laughter and clapping her hands.

---

was a fortuitous meeting" (purely accidental) and "It was a fortunate meeting" (auspicious and positive). The loss of this distinction will be unfortunate, but it's already happening, as you note. How infelicitous.

Q. This appeared on a web site: "Their search engine is faster and more accurate then anything else on the market." Aaaaargh!

A. Sedatives, please. You are referring, of course, to the semiliterate confusion between then and than: "She is heavier then her sister." "I enjoy mysteries more then I enjoy poetry." "She finished her speech, than sat down." "When the job is done, than you can have a treat." Wrong, wrong, all sadly wrong.

Q. Which letters are used more frequently in English?

A. Depending on the study, there are variant answers, but for vowels, in order of frequency, e, a, o, i, and u. For consonants, t, s, n, r, and h. The keyboard on the old linotype typesetting machines reflected this order of frequency: etaoin shrdlu.

Q. Did it ever occur to anyone that if you don't know how a word begins, you can't look it up in a dictionary?

A. Yes, but alphabetical order is firmly entrenched in dictionary construction. The problem, as you point out, is that the first letter of a word does not always look like it sounds. The following chart, which matches initial sound and spelling possibilities, appeared in my *Handbook for Basic Writers* (Prentice Hall, 1991).

Initial Sound	Possible Spelling
A as in *ace*:	a (able), ae (aerate), ai (AIDS), ei (eight).
CH as in *chips*:	ce (cello), ch (church).
E as in *even*:	ae (Aesop), e (eviction), ea (eagle) ee (eel), ei (either).
F as in *fog*:	f (feeling), ph (photography).
H as in *happy*:	h (horror), wh (who).
I as in *ice*:	ai (aisle), ay (ayatollah), ei (Eiffel Tower), i (isolation), is (island).
J as in *job*:	g (giant), j (justice).
K as in *kitten*:	c (cowboy), ch (chorus), k (kilogram), qu (queue).
KW as in *quick*:	cui (cuisine), kw (Kwangtung), qu (question).
N as in *nine*:	gn (gnat), kn (knee), n (notice), pn (pneumonia).
O as in *over*:	au (au gratin), o (opening), oa (oak), ow (owner).
R as in *rest*:	r (reading), rh (rhetoric), wr (writing).
S as in *sister*:	c (cigar), ps (psalm), s (suspect), sc (science), sz (Szechwan).
SH as in *shut*:	ch (chef), sch (Schultz), sh (shovel), su (sugar).
T as in *turn*:	pt (ptomaine), t (tension).
U as in *use*:	eu (eulogy), ew (ewe), u (usually), yu (Yugoslavia).
UH as in *up*:	a (about), o (opponent), u (ugly).
Z as in *zero*:	cz (czar), ts (tsar), x (xenon), z (zebra).

Quick Quiz
20. puteal: pertaining to a

(A) well   (B) meadow   (C) village   (D) coal mine

Q. I always thought that each phobia had its own name, but I've seen a number of different words claiming to mean "fear of cats." What's going on?

A. Sometimes variant spellings are based on transliterating an ancient word with different systems. For instance, *aelurophobia, ailurophobia,* and *elurophobia*—all meaning fear of cats—are really the same word with a whisker of difference. At other times, the spelling depends upon the language of origin. Thus, felinophobia comes to us from the Latin, galeophobia from the Greek, and gatophobia from the Spanish.

Other fears have multiple forms, too. For instance, fear of drinking alcoholic beverages may be rendered as *alcoholophobia, potophobia, dipsomanophobia,* and *methyphobia.* The only thing we have to fear is... spelling.

Q. While I was on a web site the other night, I received the warning message, "Excess Denied." That can't be right, can it?

A. I suppose it depends on the type of web site you were visiting. Don't ask, don't tell. Along with you, I would assume that some inattentive webmaster misspelled "Access Denied."

Access is a synonym for entry or approachability, whereas *excess* means a surplus, an abundance, or overindulgence. Speaking of which, some overindulgent synonyms for *excess* include *supernumerary, recrementious,* and *supererogatory.* Daunting, eh?

☞ THE GAME OF THE NAME ☜
Bambi comes from the Italian for young girl

Q. A local newscaster used this construction: "The choices run the gambit from A to Z." That just doesn't sound kosher.

A. It's not. The wrong word was used. A gambit is a maneuver, strategy, or ploy. We speak of an opening gambit in chess. Your newsie, on the other hand, should have used gamut, a complete range or extent. Someone's face might mirror a gamut of emotions, or a long-distance runner might experience the gamut of physical reactions from pain to euphoria.

Interesting sidebar: *gambit* comes from an old Italian word meaning leg. A standard opening move in wrestling was to trip your opponent.

Q. Should there be a distinction between *further* and *farther*?

A. There are good reasons to use *further* to mean additional and *farther* to refer to distance, although I will concede that many writers blur the differences. For instance, it is preferable to say, "Any further delay will bankrupt the company," and "Further suggestions may be forwarded to the pastor." Use farther in sentences such as these: "He went farther than any astronaut before him." "The farther you travel, the more exotic things become."

Answer 20: (A) well
[L. *putea*, pit]

Puteal properly means the enclosure surrounding the opening of a well, to protect persons from falling into it.

Q. Is there a name for a sentence composed entirely of two-letter words? What made me think of this was a motivational mantra: "If it is to be, it is up to me."

A. I'm not sure if there is such a term, but it's easy enough to make one up. There already is a term to describe a two-letter word; it's biliteral, according to the *Oxford English Dictionary*. It's a small step, therefore, to refer to a biliteral sentence. The term is larger than the reality it names, which reminds me of the old complaint: "Why is abbreviation such a long word?"

By the way, don't confuse *biliteral* with *bilittoral*, pertaining to two shorelines—as of a person who owns a house on Lake Michigan in Illinois and a vacation cottage on Lake Michigan in the state of Michigan.

Q. Is it worthwhile differentiating *precedents* and *precedence*?

A. Yes, even though both words share the same root, meaning "to go before."

Precedents are instances or examples that are used in later, similar situations to make a choice or judgment. Thus, lawyers and judges constantly refer to legal precedents. *Precedence* means priority or preference, often based on an assumed superiority. Ticket orders arriving first have precedence over those arriving later, and generals have precedence over privates when it comes to choosing assignments. Ironically, the pecking order in a church procession is reversed. The participants are lined up in order of precedence, with the lowly first and the highest rank of clergy last. A classic example of the last being first.

☞   WORD FACT   ☜
Many ancient hunters believed that it was unlucky to use the name of an animal that they were stalking. The bear, for instance, was variously known as the good calf (Irish), honey pig (Welsh), honey eater (Russian), and the licker (Lithuanian).

Q. From context, I gather that *fuscous* is some kind of color, but what kind?

A. Murky, at best. Some dictionaries define it as dark brownish-gray, which is about as clear as mud. Webster's Third New International bravely describes it as lighter than taupe, less strong than average chocolate, and slightly redder than mouse gray. Got it?

Q. What is the difference between bring and take?

A. Point of view is at issue here. *Bring* implies motion toward the speaker or writer; it is a synonym for *come here*. *Take* implies motion away from the writer or speaker; it is a synonym for *go there*. So a waiter takes your order and brings your food. However, from the chef's point of view, the waiter brings your order and takes your food.

Q. Should it be "If you or a friend join..." or "If you or a friend joins..."?

A. The conjunction being used makes all the difference. When parts of a compound subject are joined by OR or NOR, the verb agrees with the subject part closer to it.
Neither the teacher nor the students are here.
    [students = plural]
Neither the students nor the teacher is here.
    [teacher = sing.]

QUICK QUIZ
21. Grown or developed:

(A) pauperitic (B) burgeoned (C) marcescent (D) enervated

If you or a friend joins....
        [friend = sing.]

On the other hand, use a plural verb when the subject consists of two or more items joined by AND.
        If you and a friend join...
        Bricks and mortar go together.

Q.   "Send the results to the Director or myself," says a recent bulletin at work. Is that use of *myself* legitimate?

A.   Let's just say this: it's fairly common. Some people have an aversion to using the word *me*, perhaps in the mistaken notion that it's too blunt or egotistic. I'd prefer to see, "Send the results to the Director or to me." Using a second preposition somehow seems to make the pronoun *me* sound less harsh. Irrelevant flicker of pronoun memory: I'll always remember my Irish mother referring to my father as "himself" instead of using his name.

Q.   Which is correct: "There is a higher incidents of SARS in Asia," or "There is a higher incidence of SARS in Asia"?

A.   Go with incidence.
Incidents is the plural form of incident, an event or occurrence. *Incidence* refers to the extent or frequency with which something happens, and that is what is meant in your SARS example. You could combine them by saying, "The incidence of unpleasant incidents is increasing."

☞   BUMPER STICKER   ☜
Does the name Pavlov ring a bell?

Q. What's the difference between an araneologist and an arachnologist?

A. One is a specialist in the study of spiders, and the other is a specialist in the study of spiders. What a tangled web we weave. The route of entry into English is what's at stake here. In Latin, *aranea* means spider. In Greek, it was *arachne*. (The *-ologist* part always signifies a specialist.) It's not unusual for English to have two or more versions of the same word because of those two contributing languages. For instance, tetrad and quartet both refer to a set of four, and felinophobia and ailurophobia both mean fear of, or aversion to, cats.

Q. Can every letter in the English alphabet be silent— that is, unpronounced—given the right circumstances?

A. In conversational English, every letter of the alphabet can glide by as if it weren't even there. The -x- is silent in *faux*, the -s- is silent in *aisle*, the -g- is silent in *gnu*, the -l- is silent in *talk*, and so on. If you are speaking only of initial letters, however, some of them are never silent in that position: f, l, q, s, u, v, and x are always pronounced at the beginning of a word, even if the -q- sometimes sounds like a -k- or the -x- sometimes sounds like a -z-.

Answer 21: (B) burgeoned
[ME *burjon*, bud]

The Cherry Festival has burgeoned over the years.

Q.　How would you use the word *phaze* in a sentence?

A.　I wouldn't; there's no such word that I'm aware of, unless you're referring to the name of a heavy-metal band or an avant-garde clothing store. There is a sound-alike word *phase*, a stage of development, and then there's *faze*, a verb meaning to disturb or bother. "She's only going through a phase; don't let it faze you." Perhaps you could copyright *phazed* to mean "frazzled by your teenager's behavior."

Q.　Defending an artist accused of plagiarism, a letter-to-the-editor writer said, "Is a flower- or fruit-laden tree in front of the bay exclusionary to Mackinac Island?" That sounds like poor word choice to me.

A.　Agreed. In the right context, both *exclusionary* and *exclusive* can refer to omission, being left out: *exclusionary immigration policies; an exclusive club.* What the writer meant here was *unique, single, sole, not shared with others,* and the word that covers that is *exclusive,* as in *exclusive publishing rights.*

Q.　A local hospital recently held what it called a "health-orama." Could you comment on that *-orama* ending, which seems to be cropping up more and more often?

A.　The *-orama* suffix shows up in web-orama, Halloween-orama, food-orama, and dozens of other neologisms. It comes from the Greek *(h)orama,* view or sight, and it designates a significant display or spectacle. Probably the first English word to use it was panorama, and since then the combining form has been applied to all kinds of situations where a wide spectrum of information or offerings is a value.

Q. Quote and quotation: if they mean the same thing, why are there two of them?

A. As your eye will tell you, *quote* is an abbreviation of *quotation*. As such, many people still consider it less formal than the full word. You won't go wrong if you use the spelling *quotation* for formal situations (as in *a biblical quotation*) and *quote* for informal situations (*a George Carlin quote*). And be aware that a few diehards still maintain that *quote* must be used as a verb, never as a noun.

Q. What is the purpose of the punctuation mark that looks like a peak (^) ?

A. It's called a caret, and when it's inserted below a line, it's to add a word or term that was inadvertently left out. Above a letter, it's an accent mark. Don't confuse it with carat, a unit of weight for precious stones.

Q. Where did *kitty-corner* come from, and what does it have to do with cats?

A. It refers to a diagonal, of course, but it has nothing to do with animals. The *kitty* portion is a corruption of the original spelling, *cater*. *Cater-corner* came from the Old French *catre*, four, which was a descendant of the Latin word *quattuor*, four. So think of a box with four corners, each of which is cater-corner to another one.

QUICK QUIZ
22. factitious:

(A) literary   (B) divided   (C) thoughtful   (D) artificial

Q. Talking about a traffic ticket that she got out of, a friend of mine said that she excavated herself from a messy situation. Shouldn't that be extricated?

A. Yes, extricated is the word that she meant. *Excavate* means to remove by digging or scooping out, while *extricate* means to release from a difficulty or entanglement. She extricated herself from a problem. I think that another idiom may have led to her confusion. We sometimes say, "I dug myself out of a hole" to signify that we escaped a problem by our own devices, so she may have associated that with the digging meaning of excavate. Hollow, scoop, unearth, and mine would be synonyms for *excavate*, and release, disentangle, disengage, and untangle would serve the same purpose for *extricate*.

Q. What is the essential difference between *possible* and *probable*?

A. Spelling. Just kidding. Something *possible* is capable of happening, whether it ever does or not. Something *probable* is likely to happen, so it has more immediacy. This reminds me of another usage that teachers used to pound into our heads: *can* means that you are capable of doing something; *may* means that you have permission to do something, making it more immediately likely to happen. These two are now blurring.

☞ WORD FACT ☜

Using dictionaries and spell checkers is second nature in our day, but earlier centuries were far more casual about spelling. Here is a sentence written about King James I in the 17th century: "He was of a middle stature, more corpulent though in his clothes than in his body, yet fat enough, his cloathes being ever made large and easie..." Two ways to spell clothes in the same sentence!

Q. Not so much a question as a *tsk! tsk!* I attended a concert the other night, and the program notes read, "He is the principle conductor of the Young Musicians Symphony Orchestra."

A. That one hits a sour note. The spelling *principle* is always a noun, never an adjective, and it refers to a rule, standard, or law. What the program meant was *principal*, meaning chief or leading. Principal can also be a noun. It can refer to the head of a school or to an important player in a business, trial, sale, etc.

Q. Should it be *preventative measures* or *preventive measures*?

A. Though *preventative* is listed in some dictionaries as a variant spelling, you should stick with *preventive*, meaning intended to hinder or forestall. It can also be used as a noun meaning an obstacle. Avoid the clutter of the extra syllable.

Q. Is it *averse circumstances* or *adverse circumstances*?

A. This one gets a little tricky because both words come from the same source, a Latin word meaning *to turn*.

Generally, *averse* refers to an internal attitude: it proclaims a person's feelings against something: *"Many investors are averse to risk." "I am averse to buttermilk."* [n. aversion]

Answer 22: (D) artificial
[L. *facere*, to make]

People with factitious disorder feign or actually induce illness in themselves, typically to garner the nurturance of others.

Broadly speaking, *adverse* refers to opposition from the outside. *"Adverse circumstances can make you work harder, but adverse criticism can wear you down."* [n. adversity]

Q. Does it matter whether I use *historic* or *historical*?

A. Some casual writers use them interchangeably, but I think there's a distinction worth preserving. Use *historic* to designate something significant or important: *the historic meeting between Grant and Lee; a historic building.* Use historical to refer to <u>anything</u> from the past, significant or trivial: *historical data; historical correlation between the price of stocks and the length of hemlines.*

Q. Can *obtain* and *attain* be substituted for each other?

A. Not really, though in one meaning (to get), *attain* and *obtain* intersect. *Attain* means to achieve or accomplish. We'd say, *"She attained her goal after great effort."* We really can't substitute *obtain*. *Obtain* means to get or acquire. *"He obtained his driver's license after passing the test."* So *attain* implies striving and persistence and the passage of time, while *obtain* might simply involve the exchange of money or happen in a short period of time. *"She attained her education after years of hard work, and she obtained her degree on June 8, 2003."*

Q. Comment, please, on *affinity, penchant, proclivity,* and *propensity.*

A. You've latched onto some synonyms that are tightly connected. Depending on the dictionary consulted, the following words are used interchangeably to define the four: attraction, disposition, inclination, leaning, liking, predilection, proneness, tendency.

I'd arrange the four terms in either of two ways.

1. Ends: *affinity* and *penchant* tend toward good ends, *proclivity* and *propensity* toward bad ends.
2. Strength: *affinity* and *propensity* are slightly weaker attractions, *penchant* and *proclivity* slightly stronger.

Q. My question concerns the use of anyone or anybody, someone or somebody, everyone or everybody. Are there any general guidelines?

A. As far as I can determine, the word pairs are interchangeable. Some grammarians (such as Bryan Garner) say that the choice should be based on euphony—what sounds better in a given context.

It's not scientific, but I've always felt that the pronouns ending in -*one* are a bit more formal, and the pronouns ending in -*body* are just a tad more informal. I can picture Queen Elizabeth II asking her guests, "Is everyone having a good time?" On the other hand, my alcoholic Uncle Louie would bellow, "Ish everybuddy havin' a good time?"

At any rate, you've probably noticed that anyone, everyone, and someone appear far more frequently in print. I suppose that's what gave me the impression that the -*one* set is more formal.

☞   ALSO KNOWN AS   ☜
scarf: join with bevelled or notched ends

QUICK QUIZ
23. pertaining to abrupt changes

(A) consilient   (B) transilient   (C) dissilient   (D) emollient

---

Q. A senior center bulletin advertises a foot care clinic which, among other things, will treat callouses. Shouldn't that be calluses?

A. Not to be thin-skinned about it, but yes. Callous means either "having calluses" or "emotionally hardened." A callus is the thickened, tough area of skin itself. I think you've discovered their Achilles' heel.

Q. Recently my daughter asked me why the abbreviation No. is used for the word number even though the letter "o" is not in the word. What can you find?

A. My compliments; you have a very perceptive daughter. The Latin form of the word is the reason why that stray "o" appears. For instance, "in numero octo" would have been translated, "8 in number." Somewhere along the way, when people were looking for an abbreviation for the word, they turned to the Latin form and took its first and last letter. But here's an oddity that I hadn't thought of before. When someone decided on a plural form, nos. was chosen. What that does is slap an English plural (-s) on a Latin singular. Had they stayed with pure Latin, it should have been nis. to represent *in numeris*. Consistency, thy name is not English.

Q. Take a look at this: "Gaylord business leaders adopted the use of the peeked roofs, white stucco siding and cedar shingles about 40 years ago to promote business and establish the area as a tourist destination."

A. That explains the eerie feeling that something was staring at my back when I went into The Sugar Bowl last week. A tapering or pointed structure has a peak and may be described as peaked. A quick or surreptitious glance is a peek, and the spelling peeked is not used as an adjective, but as a past tense verb: *she peeked at the peaked roof.* A slight complication: the spelling peaked, but pronounced *pee' kid*, has a totally different meaning. If your grandmother says that you look peaked, she is probably not referring to your pointy head. She means that you have a sickly appearance.

An unanswered question: if you are addressing a Bighorn sheep perched at the top of a mountain, is it correct to say, "Peakaboo, I see ewe"?

Q. A question for you about the expression "dead of winter": Where did it come from, and how will we know when we've reached the dead of winter?

A. Most of my usual sources are silent on this one, but the *Oxford English Dictionary* was able to shed some light. The phrase refers to "the time of intensest stillness, darkness, cold, etc." The first time it was used in print, according to the OED, was in *Travels in Persia*, which came out in 1613. As to how we know when we've reached it, I suspect there's a strong subjective element. I always think of January as the dead of winter, but I suppose that the only way to tell for any given winter is in retrospect. By the way, the same use of "dead" shows up in *dead of night* and *dead of neap* (the extreme stage of neap tide—the semi-monthly lowest high tide).

☞ THE GAME OF THE NAME ☜
Bart came from an Aramaic phrase,
son of the furrowed one.

Answer 23   (B) transilient
[L. *transilire*, to leap across]

Transilient nerve fibers pass from one convolution of
the brain to another not immediately adjacent.

Q. My local paper had this: "While the cost may be substantial from the prospective of waste treatment alone, the commissioners once again failed to observe the ancillary benefit that ownership of the treatment facility could have provided."

A. I assume you're pointing to the misuse of *prospective*; it should be *perspective*. The context shows that the letter writer meant point of view, and that is covered by the word perspective. (*From a parent's perspective, drugs are a nightmare.*) Prospective refers to something that is likely to happen or is hoped for. A company will speak of prospective clients, and a school registrar will refer to prospective students.

<u>Memory Aid</u>: *per* means through, as in *through one's eyes*, and *pro* means forward or future, as in *making a proposal*. Be careful though; *pro* has other meanings, too.

Q. I recently heard a politician refer to "basic fundamental rules." Isn't that redundant?

A. No doubt about it. One dictionary defines *basic* as fundamental, and then goes on to define *fundamental* as relating to the base. So we're drowning in sameness here, which is appropriate because the root in *redundant* is a Latin word meaning wave (*unda-*). Something redundant is overflowing. Wave after wave of identical meanings wash over us. Watch for that same root in other words, among them *abundant, inundate, undulate,* and *undine.*

☞   WORD FACT   ☜

If you can't remember a word that you want to use, you are experiencing lethologica. At least, that's what I think it's called.

Q.   I like to watch vintage movies on TV, and one of the terms that comes up every so often in old western films is the expression, "you old galoot!" What is a galoot?

A.   No one seems to be certain of its origin, but we do know that in the early 19th century it was a slang term for a soldier. For some reason, by the end of that century it had come to mean a chump or an uncouth person. Eric Partridge (*A Dictionary of the Underworld*) favors an old Irish word meaning dolt as the source.

Q.   When I share the feelings of a friend, am I exhibiting sympathy or empathy?

A.   Both are admirable expressions of compassion, but empathy is a bit more encompassing. The *em-* part of empathy indicates that you get right *inside* your friend's feelings and have them become your own. The *sym-* part of sympathy shows that you feel right *along with* your friend, but perhaps in a more objective way, at least to the point of observing identity boundaries.

Q.   Impel and compel—are they interchangeable?

A.   Both contain the meaning push because of the word part *-pel-*. However, *impel* is a gentler push; it implies urging or cheerleading or non-threatening persuasion. *Compel* implies force; you're not given much choice. Your personal his-

---

QUICK QUIZ
24. sequacious

(A) humorous   (B) reckless   (C) ordinary   (D) slavish

---

tory may impel you toward a military career; a compulsory draft would compel you to become a soldier.

Dispel, expel, propel, and *repel* share the same root, while *-puls-* is found in *compulsive, expulsed, propulsion,* and *repulsive.*

Q. An article in a music magazine spoke of flawed sound tracts in CDs and why they happen. Doesn't *tract* refer to acreage?

A. Dischord hovers in the air, as it were. The writer obviously meant sound <u>tracks</u>. This goes back to earlier recording procedures when grooved tracks in vinyl were used to reproduce sound. Now, even though it's done with pits or bumps, it still involves one long, continuous track. I'm told that it can be 3 and a half miles long! Tract covers meanings ranging from an area of land to anatomical features to housing developments to pamphlets.

Q. Which one is correct? "I can't stand his being a good-for-nothing lowlife" or "I can't stand him being a good-for-nothing lowlife."

A. This one is another grammar snake pit, with critics hissing from both sides. Most of us were taught that the first version—with the pronoun *his* in the possessive case—is the correct one. But the fact is that for hundreds of years, the version using the objective case *him* has existed side by side. It is not unusual to find the **very same author** using both versions in a single chapter. Lewis Carroll, James Boswell, George Eliot, Charles Dickens, William Thackeray, Flannery O'Connor and many more are cited in *Merriam-Webster's Concise Dictionary of English Usage* (2002). Take a look at the article "Possessive with Gerund" in that source. Broadly speaking, using *his* puts the emphasis on the following gerund or noun; using *him* puts the emphasis on the individual, not his or her act. It comes to this: if you make a choice based on emphasis in a given sentence or based on the euphony involved, half the critics will say you're right and half will say you're wrong. It doesn't get any better than that.

Q.   Is there any difference in meaning between *sub-* and *hypo-* when used as word parts?

A.   No. Both mean *under*, but while *sub-* came from Latin, *hypo-* owes its origin to Greek. Doublets such as these account for the large word hoard in our language; compare hypodermic and subcutaneous, for example. From these roots come some interesting words: subapical, subjacent, sublittoral, hypocorism, hypopnia, and hyposthenia. Head for those unabridged dictionaries!

Q.   Drastic and dramatic: how distinct are they?

A.   Something drastic always has a negative connotation. Doom and upheaval are just around the corner; it's a twitchy word. In contrast, something dramatic can be positive and desirable, such as a dramatic entrance to the Oscar Awards ceremony, or a dramatic breakthrough in cancer research. Even when they come close in meaning (*drastic budget cuts* or *dramatic budget cuts*), the first still has an edge to it, while the second serves more as an attention-getter.

Q.   When a word comes from someone's name, what's that called?

A.   An eponym is a word derived from someone's name. Sometimes the connection is dubious, but most of them can be historically verified. For instance, the heimlich maneuver

---

Answer 24   (D) slavish
[L. *sequere*, to follow]

The sequacious nature of her devotion led to instances of abuse.

---

is named after Dr. Henry Jay Heimlich, a caesarian section is named after Julius Caesar, the dahlia is named after Swedish botanist Anders Dahlia, and the diesel engine is named after Rudolph Diesel. We get gerrymander from Elbridge Gerry, schrapnel from Lieutenant General Henry Shrapnel, August from Augustus Caesar, and boycott from Charles C. Boycott.

Many people believe that the term *hooker* is derived from the name of Civil War General Joseph Hooker. However, dictionaries indicate that the word has the same derivation as *hooker* in the sense of "one that hooks," and in fact the OED2 shows a use of the term in 1845 in N. E. Eliason, *Tarheel Talk*: "If he comes by way of Norfolk he will find any number of pretty Hookers in the Brick row not far from French's hotel."

Crapper is widely believed to have come from the name of a 19th century plumber named Thomas Crapper. However, the word apparently derives from the word *crap*, which is found all the way back in Middle English.

Q.   A Carnival Cruise ad boasts, "The meals are inclusive..." Does that pass muster?

A.   I'm afraid it doesn't even pass the mustard; the word *included* should be used. Inclusive means comprehensive, taking everything within its scope: *An inclusive survey of vacation travelers; staterooms one to ten, inclusive.*

Included means taken in as a part or member; contained as an element: *The meals are included in the cruise price.*

Q.   Which is correct: *"His symphony is composed of five movements"* or *"His symphony is comprised of five movements"*?

A.   Short answer: never write or say *is comprised of.* Long answer: Comprise means to include; compose means to make by putting parts together. So saying *"...is comprised of"* is like saying *"...is included of."* Here are two guidelines to follow:

1. The whole **comprises** (includes) the parts.
The United States comprises 50 individual states.
The movie A.I. comprises three sections.
The federal government comprises three separate branches. Substitute "includes" to insure that the correct word really is "comprises."

2. The parts **compose** (add together to create) the whole.
The United States is composed of 50 individual states.
The movie A.I. is composed of three sections.
The federal government is composed of three separate branches.

Q. My sister is an artist, and she told me that camel hair brushes don't come from camels. So why the name?

A. This one gets a bit complicated. First of all, an art supply house in Florida (Rex Art) says that "camel hair is an all-encompassing term for a variety of animal hairs, none of which are camel, used alone or in combinations to create brushes. Hairs commonly used in camel hair brushes include ox, goat, squirrel and pony hair." Then why the name? Mary Bellis of *About.com* says that they are named after the inventor, Mr. Camel. *The Facts on File Encyclopedia of Word and Phrase Origins* gives the name as Kemul. Both fail to give a citation.

QUICK QUIZ
25. turpitude

(A) sluggishness (B) wickedness (C) happiness (D) quickness

On the other hand, there are brushes made from actual camel hair; they are used throughout the foundry indus-
try for cleaning and coating molds, and they are used for
hobbies and crafts. But artists are unlikely to use 100% camel
hair brushes. Artist Marion Boddy-Evans of *About.com* says
that "camel hair is unsuitable for brushes because it's too
woolly."

Q. I work with young single mothers. I have to write
up a short case log for each client visited. My supervisor com-
plains that my reports are dull. She says my writing is te-
dious. Can you suggest a quick fix to get her off my back?

A. I sympathize, Heather, because I know work-re-
lated writing usually focuses on details and technicalities and
sacrifices style. But there are a few things you can do to make
short reports—I take that to mean three to five paragraphs—
more interesting.

First, **vary your sentence types**—not just the length, but
the type. Let's say that you've written: *"The client's infant son
cries all night. She is frustrated. She needs training intervention."*
Those sentences are clear, which is valuable in itself, but they
are all simple sentences (independent clause only) and they
establish a dull rhythm.

1. Try mixing in some compound sentences (two simple
sentences tied together with *and/but/or/nor/for/so/yet*).
You could write, for instance,"The *client's infant son cries
all night, so she is frustrated. She needs training intervention."*
2. Try mixing in some complex sentences (independent
clause + one or more dependent clauses): *"The client is
frustrated because her infant son cries all night. She needs
training intervention."*
3. Occasionally, you'll want to mix those two together
in a long sentence called a compound-complex sentence:
*The client needs training intervention because her infant son
cries all night and she is frustrated.*

Second, **use transitional words** to connect thoughts. Here are some words for different situations. You would never use them <u>all</u> in one report, by the way.

1. To keep an idea going: *above all, also, besides, first second/third, furthermore, in addition, meanwhile, moreover, next*

2. To explain an idea: *for example, for instance, in other words, that is*

3. To show an opposing view: *however, in contrast, on the other hand, otherwise*

4. To end an idea: *as a result, finally, in conclusion, in summary, last, therefore.* So you could write, *Because her infant son cries all night, the client is frustrated. Consequently, she needs training intervention.*

Finally, always give priority to the **active voice**. Instead of saying, *A complaint was generated by the client*, say, *The client complained.*

Q. Isn't there a discrepancy between the names of our calendar months and their sequence?

A. Yes, and you can blame the Romans. Since they had 10 months in their calendar and we have 12, there are now some inconsistencies permanently built into the names.

- January: named for the god Janus, god of gates, doorways, and beginnings in general.
- February: the month of purification, the name taken from the Latin *februa*, expiatory offerings.

Answer 25   (B) wickedness
[L. *turpis*, shameful]

The minister devoted his career to stamping out moral turpitude.

- March: named for Mars, the god of war.
- April: named for Aprhrodite, the goddess of love and beauty.
- May: named for the goddess Maia, the mother of Hermes.
- June: named for Juno, the goddess of women, marriage, childbirth, and the moon.
- July: named for Julius Caesar.
- August: named for Augustus Caesar.
- September: the 7th month in the Roman calendar.
- October: the 8th month in the Roman calendar.
- November: the 9th month in the Roman calendar.
- December: the 10th month in the Roman calendar.

Q.   What is the difference between dialect and jargon?

A.   Dialect is usually associated with a geographic region. It involves features such as vowel sounds, diphthong values, speed of talking, clipped or unclipped words, sentence structure, and vocabulary. Note that it's not too difficult for the average person to identify broadly where someone came from (California, Deep South, Maine, etc.).

Jargon, rather than being limited to a specific region, is usually the property of particular professions, hobbies, pursuits, and so on. Generally, a specialized vocabulary is the strongest feature of jargon. Speakers will retain their regional accents, but they will share a common technical vocabulary. When it is designed merely to exclude outsiders, jargon is subject to ridicule; when it is designed to allow professionals to communicate efficiently and accurately, it serves a useful purpose.

The word vernacular covers the everyday language spoken by a people as opposed to a more literary language, but it sometimes is a synonym for dialect (*the vernaculars of New York City*) and sometimes a synonym for jargon (*the legal vernacular*).

Q. A news report the other day quoted a member of Parliament as saying that he contemned Tony Blair's Iraq policy. Is that a British variant on condemn—something like their spelling of civilisation as opposed to our spelling of civilization?

A. No, contemn is a word in its own right, the verb form of contempt. To contemn is fairly high on the dislike scale, probably somewhere just under full-bore loathing. It is an emotional response akin to detest and despise. On the other hand, we can condemn a person or a policy with no show of emotion. A good judge, I suppose, could condemn a convicted murderer without any personal animosity.

Q. In prehistoric times, when we used typewriters instead of computers, one of the keyboard training exercises was, "The quick brown fox jumps over a lazy dog." Does the computer generation still use this?

A. If web sites are any indication, they have gone light years beyond that standard exercise. A sentence that uses all 26 letters of the alphabet—preferably in the shortest possible space—is known as a pangram, from the Greek *pan-*, all, and *gram-*, writing. I have seen some sentences that use each letter only once, but the words involved are archaic, or Welsh, or in other ways incomprehensible. Most of the time, to create an intelligible sentence, thirty or more letters will be used. Here are some examples.

QUICK QUIZ
26. rasorial: referring to

(A) chickens (B) cockroaches (C) bats (D) horses

- We promptly judged antique ivory buckles for the next prize.
- The five boxing wizards jump quickly.
- Pack my box with five dozen liquor jugs.
- Sixty zippers were quickly picked from the woven jute bag.
- Waltz, bad nymph, for quick jigs vex is better still.

To see hundreds, if not thousands more, just type "pangram" into your favorite search engine query form. Most hits will be word puzzle sites.

Q. Raining cats and dogs—where did that come from?

A. It means a torrential downpour, and it seems to have been around since the 18th century. The most likely explanation is that after a heavy rainstorm, gutters would overflow with garbage, sewage, and dead animals left by the side of the street, all of which would be swept along by the torrent. 18th century hygiene left a lot to be desired. Frontier America would have referred to such a downpour as a gully washer.

Q. During a press conference about that October 2003 Staten Island Ferry crash, a transportation official declined to call it a collision. He stated that it takes two moving objects to justify that word, and that this incident should be called an allision since only the ferry was moving.

A. In your phone call to the radio program, *Words to the Wise*, you went on to speculate that the *-col-* in collision means mutual or together with, and this may have technically prompted him to use the obscure word allision instead. I was able to track it down in the *Oxford English Dictionary*, and esoteric is the name for it, since the examples given date from the 17th and 18th centuries. "The action of dashing against or striking with violence upon" is the definition that the OED gives for allision. While it is not explicitly stated, the reference seems to be to a single moving object. I marvel at the official's precise word choice. As it turns out, he is backed by *Black's Law Dictionary*. There is also the obsolete verb *allide*, formed from the prefix *ad-*, toward or against.

Q. Where did the phrase *checkered past* come from, as in, "She had a checkered past"?

A. While it doesn't mean that the lady in question sat around playing board games, there *is* a linguistic connection.

Checker, meaning chessboard, came into the English language from the French *eschec* in the 14th century. In time, the meaning expanded to any pattern resembling the squares of a chessboard because of color or shading. It wasn't then a huge step to apply it to anything with variations or contrasting elements. So, that lady with the checkered past has both good things and bad things on her personal record, light and shadow. Allied phrases are *shady past* or *spotted history*.

Sidebar: Lori Allen has a clever pun on *Britannica.com*: "Just what is that black-and-white checked scarf Arafat always wears with his fatigues? The Palestinian *kaffiyya* has become an item loaded with semiotics, more emblem than accessory. It doesn't have a checkered past, exactly, but certainly a long and varied one."

☞   ALSO KNOWN AS   ☜
tingle: metal clip supporting roof glass or slates

Answer 26   (A) chickens
[L. *radere*, to scrape or shave]

Chickens and similar birds scratch the ground for food; they are rasorial.

Q.   I'm sending along a study for you to share with your listeners which claims that English-speaking countries have more dyslexics than other countries.

A.   This fascinating study appeared in the March 2001 journal *Science*. The essence is this: Italian has 33 sounds that are spelled with only 25 letters or letter combinations. French has 32 sounds that are written in about 250 letter combinations. English has 40 sounds that are spelled with more than 1,100 combinations. The complexity of sounds in English, say the authors, may explain why there are twice as many identified dyslexics in English-speaking countries.

Q.   Is it better to be a skeptic or a cynic?

A.   Far be it from me to mess with your coping mechanism. I'll just talk about the words themselves. Originally, the Skeptics were a group of Greek philosophers who lived around the 3rd century B.C. To them, it was irrational to swallow dogmatic proclamations or absolutes, so they cultivated the practice of questioning everything; they were skeptical. The term originally came from a Greek word meaning *to examine*. The Cynics, also a Greek school of philosophers, thought that the pursuit of virtue was all that mattered, but they seem to have been quick to question the virtue and motives of others; they were cynical. That negatively-charged word, oddly enough, came from a Greek word meaning *dog*. It seems that their esteemed leader, Diogenes of Sinope, used to bark in public. Don't ask.

What grabs my peripheral attention is how dogs have been maligned over the centuries. If I were a canine, I'd be cynical, too, because of *dirty dog, dog eat dog, dog in the manger, not a dog's chance, sick as a dog, sly dog, die like a dog, dog it, go to the dogs, throw to the dogs, dog-faced, barking up the wrong tree,* and a kennel full of other figures of speech.

Q. Where does "grass widow" come from?

A. As happens with a significant number of figures of speech, there is some obscurity here. First of all, there is more than one definition:

- A woman who is divorced or separated from her husband.
- A woman whose husband is temporarily absent.
- An abandoned mistress.
- The mother of a child born out of wedlock.

The last definition seems to be the oldest (1528), and it alludes to a bed of grass or hay–in other words, a non-marital bed. The vulgar phrase *a roll in the hay* would be related. Later extensions or explanations referred to someone put out to pasture, to Anglo-Indian wives sent to hill stations for the summer, to prospectors' wives set up in boarding houses while the men mined, and so on, but they don't seem to hold up. In modern times, according to the joke, a grass widow is the wife of an avid golfer.

☞ WORD FACT ☜

At the current rate of destruction, only 10 percent of the world's 6,000 languages and dialects will survive the next 100 years.

QUICK QUIZ
27. The word part *cromny-* is used to describe which vegetable?

(A) carrot (B) onion (C) green pepper (D) sweet potato

Q. Is there a word for reading meaning into a text rather than drawing out what is actually there? I have a professor who distorts everything (as I see it) according to his religious beliefs. He couldn't read a phone book without finding traces of original sin.

A. The word is eisegesis (Greek *eis-*, into, + *hegeisthai*, to lead). It is the opposite of exegesis (*ex-*, out of), a fancy name for critical analysis.

Q. Where does the term *hit the ground running* come from?

A. Many commentators, including William Safire, believe that it originated in WWII as instructions to military forces. Here are some of the possibilities proffered:

- instructions to paratroopers for the moment of landing;
- instructions to Sailors and Marines exiting from a beach landing craft;
- instructions to British assault forces landing in gliders;
- instructions to hoboes jumping from a moving train;
- instructions to Pony Express riders at horse-changing stations;
- instructions to rodeo bronco and bull riders;
- a reference to the work of Edward James Muggeridge, 19th century collodion process photographer, whose multiple camera experiments proved that at some point in its stride, all four feet of a race horse are off the ground.

114

I don't know which is historically accurate, but I must admit to being swayed by Spielberg's *Saving Private Ryan* and its unforgettable imagery.

Q. Here's a clip from a local newspaper. "...There's quite a cult following for morel mushrooms," [a housing developer] said. "We've had mitologists and botany professors from colleges and universities on our outings, and people who don't know whether morels grow in trees."

A. My wife and I like to hunt morels, so I know you're reacting to the word *mitologists*. The proper name for someone who specializes in mushrooms is *mycologist*, from *myco-*, meaning fungus. A mitologist would be an expert on mites, just as a miticide would be a substance or compound capable of killing mites. Perhaps it was a cult of nitpickers.

Q. Whenever I drive through Michigan's Upper Peninsula, I get the impression that all they sell is cement lawn ornaments and pasties, those meat-filled pies. So I'm wondering, where did the word *pasty* come from?

A. Don't go dissing da Yoopers, eh? Pasty comes to us from Great Britain, where these seasoned meat or fish turnovers were popular with miners; it was a self-contained meal. A variation of the word (and the food) shows up in Middle English and in Old French. In turn, they came from the Latin *pastatum* (pastry-wrapped meat), which tracks back to pasta.

Answer 27
(B) onion   [Gr. *cromnmon*, onion]

Cromnyomancy was a form of divination that
studied the layers of an onion.

So it turns out that the words pasty, pasta, paté, patty, and paste are all cousins. By the way, if you don't want to appear declassé, don't pronounce the -*a*- in pasty with a long sound (pay'-stee). That's something worn by ecdysiasts. Instead, give it the value of the -*a*- in *after*.

Q. If English owes so much to German, French, Latin and other languages, why doesn't it have separate gender forms for masculine, feminine, and neuter as they do? For instance, instead of a genderless *the* (the boy, the girl, the wall), we find *der*, *die*, and *das* in German, *el*, *la*, and *lo* in Spanish, etc.

A. English is a Germanic language, an offshoot of the western branch of the Germanic family. It took root in Britain after the invasions of the Angles, the Saxons, and the Jutes— all Germanic tribes—in the 5th and 6th centuries. In its earliest form, Old English **did** have separate gender spellings, even for the articles. It was a much more complicated language than it is today. If history had been different, present-day English would compare to German much as modern Dutch compares to German.

But because of Scandinavian invasions that left their mark on the language, and because of fragmented dialects all over Britain, changes were inevitable. The simplification process exploded after the Norman invasion in 1066. For a little over a century, English was basically a **spoken** language only, as Norman French dominated royal and legal affairs, and Latin dominated religious affairs. Lacking the precision and visual stability of written language, English dropped all kinds of inflections, including different spellings to express gender. In modern English, gender tags survive principally in a few pronouns (he/she/it) and in the endings of a handful of nouns (host/hostess, tailor/seamstress, prince/princess, waiter/waitress), but even they are disappearing.

Q. Our local YMCA is considering building a full-scale swimming facility right next to school district property. The superintendent of schools, learning of the plans, had this to say: "The YMCA program is really contiguous with what we do. I think it would be a positive partnership for the school and the Y." What did he mean by contiguous?

A. In all honesty, I'm not quite sure. *Contiguous* is a word used primarily to describe physical objects that are in actual contact, though it can also mean *next or near in time or sequence*. There are contiguous angles in geometry, contiguous row houses in a city such as Philadelphia, and contiguous states, such as Michigan and Indiana. So while the geographic sites will be contiguous, it makes no sense to say that the programs or services will be contiguous.

He could have meant *complementary* (mutually supportive). Or perhaps he was searching for the phrases *compatible with* or *consistent with*. Possibly, the word *congruous* (in agreement or harmony) was on his mind. But *contiguous* simply doesn't fit.

QUICK QUIZ
28. macilent:

(A) sticky   (B) chewable   (C) thin   (D) cutting

Q. It's been a long time since I was in school, but my teachers hammered the principal parts of verbs into my head, so I was appalled to read the misused forms in this story:

Man found in water-filled ditch laid down next to car

(AP)—A man whose car skidded off a slushy rural road was found dead in a water-filled ditch, authorities said.

According to the Sheriff, [the driver] left his vehicle and laid down near the vehicle. The county received about 6 inches of heavy, wet snow on Tuesday, he said.

The vehicle, which had three wheels on the roadway and one off, was turned off and the door closed, [the sheriff] said.

"He laid down in an inch or two of water. It was very shallow. It wasn't enough to cover the body," the Sheriff reported. "I can't explain why. I wouldn't even try."

[The driver] was alone at the time of his death, according to the Sheriff. Investigators have not been able to determine where was coming from or where he was going. Foul play is not suspected.

A. According to the verbs used in the story, authorities had better reopen the investigation pronto; the man was murdered. Here's why.

First, *LAY* means to place something or to put something in place, and its principal parts are *lay, laid, laid*. When you use this verb, there are always at least **two** items or people involved: one to place, and another to be placed. Thus, *I laid my keys on the kitchen counter. The murderer laid the victim in a ditch.*

Second, *LIE* means to rest, to recline, to assume a horizontal position, and its principal parts are *lie, lay, lain*. It is something that a person does **all by himself or herself**. Thus, *I lay on my bed sobbing after she died. For some unknown reason, the man lay in a water-filled ditch.*

So a man **laid** down next to car [headline] had to be placed there by someone else. This contradicts the observation that he was alone at the time of his death.

118

Is this too picky? No, there is a real difference in meaning, and a reporter needs to learn that. The word *lay* must replace *laid* in all three instances. End of Minute Mystery.

Q. A news story read, "The forum spurned the formation of a community task force which will investigate ways of reopening the resort." Wouldn't that mean they rejected the idea?

A. It certainly would, since spurn means precisely that. The writer should have used *spurred*, which means to urge forward or goad, originally applied to a horse and rider.

Q. A headline proclaims, "Attempted antique store thief faces life in prison." Now, I've heard of attempted theft, but never an attempted thief.

A. Right on target. We can have an unsuccessful thief or a bungling thief or a would-be thief, but the word *attempted* has to be applied to the action—the theft. The word comes from Latin: *ad-*, toward + *temptare*, to test.

☞   BUMPER STICKER   ☜
A plateau is a high form of flattery

Answer 28   (C) thin
[L. *macilentus*, thin or shriveled]

Twiggy, a British fashion model, was infamous
for her macilent appearance.

Q. I've heard the story that the word *golf* was given to the game because all the other four-letter words were already taken, but where did it really come from?

A. The word shows up as early as 1457 in Scotland to describe the game. *The Oxford English Dictionary* says that it was thought to be an alteration of a Dutch word, *colf*, which designated a stick or club, but it casts doubt on that story and opts for "of obscure origin" instead.

Here are some golf terms that you will find nowhere else, primarily because I made them up. They are my attempt to raise the vocabulary level above the four letter limit. In all cases, they refer to the ball's direction. The *-tropic* ending (Greek) means seeking, and the meaning of each opening root is revealed in the definition of its word.

- weeds/rough: runcotropic
- water: hydrotropic
- sand: psammotropic
- trees: dendrotropic
- grass/fairway: graminotropic

"Golf is a good walk spoiled." -Mark Twain

Q. Does the word gullible have anything to do with seagulls? They don't seem to be very smart birds.

A. Not directly. Most experts seem to think that *gull* comes from a Breton word meaning weeping. It is thought to be onomatopoeia, a word that imitates the sound of what it describes. But there was another, separate word *gull* that was popular during Elizabethan times. It referred to a person easy to fool, a mark. Based on the Latin word *gula*, throat, the idea was that such people would swallow anything, and that's where *gullible* came from. But some commentators point out that since seagulls will swallow anything thrown at them, this may have reinforced the image. Quite a flap.

Q. What is meant by a dangling modifier?

A. First, a basic principle: to achieve clear writing, when a word or phrase or clause describes another part of a sentence, it must be attached to that part clearly and logically. A dangling modifier is not clearly attached to what it describes, either because of physical separation or illogical assumption. Here's an example: *Having thrown the frisbee high in the air, the dog leaped up and snatched it.* It sounds as if the dog both threw and caught the disc, doesn't it? That's because the first part of the sentence isn't clearly attached to what it modifies. You'd have to rewrite it thus: *After I threw the frisbee high in the air, the dog leaped up and snatched it.* Dangling or misplaced modifiers can be unintentionally hilarious, as these samples sent in by listeners indicate.

- Pressing the button, the elevator went down to the basement.
- Driving like a maniac, the deer was hit and killed.
- Left alone in the house, the lightning scared the child.
- With his tail held high, my father led his prize bull around the arena.
- We saw firefighters fighting fires that suffered heat exhaustion.
- I saw the dead dog driving down the interstate.
- By the age of ten, both of Dana's parents had died.
- Oozing slowly across the table, Marvin watched the salad dressing.
- Hidden behind the billboard, the motorists could not see the policeman.

QUICK QUIZ
29. dried up:

(A) embrocated (B) desiccated (C) manducated (D) corticated

- Coming out of the market, the bananas fell on the pavement.
- She handed out brownies to the children stored in tupperware.

Q. Why is an attempt to distract someone from an issue called a red herring?

A. It seems to have arisen from hunting. To train hounds, their keepers would drag a dead cat or fox or sack of red herring three or four miles and then set the dogs on the scent to see how well they would do. So says a description from 1686. In our times, animal rights activists have dragged sacks of decaying fish through the fields and woods just before a hunt to lead the hounds away from the fox. Evidently, it's an overpowering smell. There is even the suggestion that escaped criminals may have used the same ruse to confuse pursuing bloodhounds. Does that sound fishy?

Q. I heard someone use the word truckalent on a political talk show last Sunday, but I can't find it in the dictionary. I'd like to know what it means.

A. The sound confused you. It's spelled truculent, and it refers to opposition filled with anger and ferocity bordering on the savage. A strong word, from the Latin *trux*, fierce.

Q. I recently heard a commentator refer to "tinkling the ivories." I always thought that the cliché was "tickling the ivories." What's your take?

A. I'm with you, both as to the observation that it's a cliché and that the word is tickling. It refers to piano playing (ivory keys in the old days) and the light touch that a good player develops. I suppose that the word tinkle might on occasion refer to the quality of sound (tinkling notes), a reflection of the metallic noise of striking bells, although that's a bit of a reach except for the high notes of a piano. And if someone like Liberace placed a candelabra on top of the piano, I suppose we could say that the reflected light was "twinkling the ivories." And, of course, a piano tuner would tinker with the strings and strikers, while a backsurge on an electric piano might tingle the ivories... *STOP ME!*

Q. I have noticed a number of words that have a negative form, but no positive form. I'm thinking about words such as unkempt or disgruntled. Any thoughts?

A. There are a fair number in common use, and they have often been the subject of verbal play. I have a vague memory of a Three Stooges routine where Curly shouts, "I am, TOO, couth!" Many of these words once had a positive form which has dropped out of sight. Unkempt means disheveled in appearance; the word kempt (1050 A.D.) referred to combed hair. An uncouth person is crude or unrefined; a couth person (1350 A.D.) was agreeable and pleasant. Something ineffable is unutterable; something effable (1637 A.D.) could be expressed in words. An ungainly person is clumsy; a gainly person (1855 A.D.) was graceful and tactful. Michael Quinion refers to these orphans as unpaired words, and you may read an article about them on his web site, World Wide Words. A classic humorous essay about lost positives entitled

---

Answer 29   (B) desiccated
[L. *siccus*, dry]

The desiccated remains of a mummy
were found in the tomb.

"How I Met My Wife" (by Jack Winter) appeared in the July 25, 1994, edition of the New Yorker. It begins, "It had been a rough day, so when I walked into the party I was very chalant, despite my efforts to appear gruntled and consolate. I was furling my wieldy umbrella for the coat check when I saw her standing alone in a corner. She was a descript person, a woman in a state of total array. Her hair was kempt, her clothing shevelled, and she moved in a gainly way."

Q. Please accept my contribution to your Jumbled Journalism Department:

(AP) "The Taliban's Bakhtar news agency said Abdul Haq was executed because he was spaying for Britain and the United States."

A. Thus proving once again that those who live by the sword shall die by the sword.

Q. I know that a palindrome reads the same backward and forward, but is there a special name for words that can be turned upside down? I'm thinking of MOM, which becomes WOW when flipped.

A. The curious things I have learned while doing this program. As it turns out, there _is_ a subgenre of that nature called ambigrams. This refers to a word or words that can be read in more than one way or from more than a single vantage point, such as both right side up and upside down. The word MOW is a natural ambigram; it reads the same upside down and backwards as right-side up.

Puzzle and word game sites have been an education to me. Evidently, there are many types of palindromes, based on rotation, reflection, or chains. **Letter** palindromes can be read in reverse letter by letter: _a man, a plan, a canal — Panama._ **Word** palindromes can be read in reverse word by word: _you can cage a swallow, can't you, but you can't swallow a cage, can_ *you?* Another clever one is *Fall leaves after leaves fall*. **Mirrored** palindromes are graphically reversible: *bid*. The word *pip* is a good illustration of variations. Flip it upside down, and you have *did*, an ambigram. Swing that around mirror fashion, and you have *bib*.

There are art and decorative forms based on the use of elaborately drawn ambigrams.

See http://www.ambigram.com/gallery/

Q. Short of using spray paint, I can't picture the scene described in a recent [local newspaper] article: "District 5 Commissioner Robert Hawley rose his hand to nominate Watkoski for the position of chairman."

A. Ah, yes, a rose by any other name. The verb *rise* — and its past tense *rose*—cannot take a direct object; it is intransitive. "Smoke rises" or "I rose from my chair" or "Out on the lawn there arose such a clatter...," but I can't rise my hand, and neither could the commissioner. Another verb is needed, this one transitive: *raise* and its past tense *raised*. I can "raise a ruckus" or she can "raise a point for consideration" or you can "raise your eyebrows" or the commissioner could have "raised his hand."

Sidebar: two allied words share the same sound but have different spellings and meanings. To raise a barn is to construct it; to raze a barn is to tear it down. A variant spelling for raze is rase, but it's old enough to be considered archaic, so it's better to avoid it.

QUICK QUIZ
30. Reluctant to yield; stubborn

(A) renitent   (B) morigerous   (C) ductile   (D) tractable

Q. Here's another example of what I believe to be spellcheckeritis: "Long before he was ready for it, he was thrust into the roll of father."

A. Right. Those computer programs aren't very good at handling subtle context. He was thrust into a role, of course, just as an actor takes on a role in a play or film. And it's an egg roll, not an egg role, as I have seen on a menu. You just have to row with the punches.

Q. My computer grammar checking program keeps scolding me for using the passive voice. What's the big deal?

A. The active voice of a verb (in which the subject is *doing* something) usually comes across as more direct, more vigorous, and less cluttered. The passive voice (in which the subject is *acted upon*) sometimes seems hesitant, evasive, or muddy.

Active	Passive
The dog bit me.	I was bitten by the dog.
Cars need gasoline.	Gasoline is needed by cars.
I hate spinach.	Spinach is hated by me.

Three features mark this transition:
(1) The subject in the active voice becomes the object of the preposition *by* in the passive voice.
(2) The object in the active voice becomes the subject in the passive voice.
(3) The verb in the active voice picks up a helping or auxiliary verb as it switches to the passive voice.

But the passive voice is not always inferior. Sometimes we need to emphasize the object, not the subject, and sometimes the subject isn't even known.

- The synagogue has been vandalized five times this year.
- In the last decade, home computers have been purchased at a phenomenal rate.
- My new car was stolen yesterday.

So I'd say appreciate the friendly help from your computer, but don't hesitate to override it when circumstances warrant.

Q. Here's one for your Clunker of the Day: "She insists that passed experience is not necessarily a predictor of the future."

A. It is a clunker. **Passed** experience would have been *avoided* experience, as in, "I let it go by and didn't participate at all." **Past** experience was meant here – experience from times gone by. Confusing the two spellings has also led to "I walked passed his house today." So past has two meanings. As a noun, it refers to time gone by. As a preposition, it means beyond: *past noon, past his house, past the point of compromise.*

Q. Aside from "write about what you know," which all English teachers urge, what advice can you give about nonfiction writing?

A. I love these open-ended questions, but I'd need an entire book to answer that one. Writing is a juggling act; a writer has to keep many things spinning simultaneously. But

---

Answer 30   (A) renitent
[L. *reniti*, to struggle against]

In this matter, he was renitent; he refused
to give in or even to compromise.

---

let me mention three considerations that are sometimes given short shrift. First, never lose sight of your **audience**. They have a major role in shaping what you have to say and how you burnish it. Use questions such as these as guidelines:

- What does my audience already know about the subject?
- What do I think they *should* know or believe about my subject?
- What do they already know about me and my credentials?
- What do I *want* them to know about me or my specific angle?
- Do they have contrary attitudes that I need to overcome?

Second, keep your **purpose** sharply in mind as you write. Ask yourself

- Do I want to explain something about the subject?
- Do I want to express something about myself or stay in the background?
- Do I want to persuade my audience to *do* some thing or simply to believe?
- Do I want to learn something by inviting readers' responses?
- What one strong outcome do I desire after people have read my piece?

Finally, strictly control your **tone**, the attitude that shows through in your words. Being formal or informal, serious or humorous, magisterial or inquiring—these must always be matters of deliberate choice. Try using these considerations to set your tone:

- Does this assignment place me in the role of teacher or leader?

- Does this assignment place me in the role of an equal?
- Does this assignment place me in the role of a learner or disciple?
- Is this a formal or a relaxed situation?
- Will humor dishonor my topic or alienate some of my readers?
- Should I speak from the head or from the heart?

APT advice: audience, purpose, tone.

Q. A number of books and articles have been published in the last few years that discuss birth order and how it affects human behavior. Over and over, I encounter the animal term "pecking order." Why apply that to humans?

A. I think it's just a case of using a well-known and handy metaphor out of convenience. As you know, in the mid 1900s, there were many studies charting the hierarchy that naturally evolves in barnyard fowl. Quite literally, pecking other birds was an outward sign of superiority, particularly when they did not peck back. It's not a big step to apply that concept to human hierarchy. If it were expressed as a simile, which overtly uses the words *like* or *as*, it might not sneak up on us or look as inappropriate: "The chain of command in human hierarchy is *like* the pecking order established amongst flocks of birds." An irrelevant aside: Did you ever notice how badly birds fare in some figures of speech? *That's for the birds.*

QUICK QUIZ
31. causing delay

(A) opprobrious (B) dilatory (C) ineffable (D) mordant

She eats like a bird. Stop pecking at your food. Birdbrain! Give someone the bird.

Q. Is there a patron saint for writers?

A. There are a few, in fact, but the one name that appears consistently in books and online is St. Francis de Sales. Bishop of Geneva (d. 1622), he wrote several books and many pamphlets explaining his theological positions. What surprises me is that St. Augustine of Hippo or St. Thomas Aquinas was not designated as patron of authors. Both were prodigious writers who had significant historical impact. But then, I didn't expect to find a patron saint for arms dealers, either — St. Adrian of Nicomedia.

Q. There's an old cliché that a good news story should answer the five W's. True?

A. It's still useful, as long as you throw in <u>how</u>, too. And you don't have to be a reporter to use questions as prompts; other writers find them useful, too. Some samples:

- WHO: Who is this person? Who likes this thing? Who does this? Who gains from this? Who will suffer because of this? Who are the experts? Who controls it?
- WHAT: What is it? What does it do? What kinds are there? What happened? What is its purpose? What is it made of? What can people do with it or to it?
- WHERE: Where did it come from? Where can I find it? Where does it work best? Where will it end up? Where did it go? Where is it used most?

- WHEN: When did it happen? When can I use it? When is it dangerous? When will it be over? When will it change? When should it begin?
- WHY: Why do people do it? Why did it happen? Why are there so many? Why is it a problem? Why is it good? Why doesn't it get better? Why doesn't it work?
- HOW: How does it work? How can you do it? How often does it happen? How is it like or unlike similar things?

Q. Is there a technical term for the slanted line that appears in constructions such as, "plants and/or animals"?

A. There's a technical term for every symbol ever to mark paper. This one is frequently referred to as a slash, which isn't very technical. But then it's also called a virgule [L. *virga*, rod] or a solidus [L. *solidus*, unbroken]. It has become an integral component of web addresses: seniors.tcnet.org/index.html

<u>Warning:</u> notice that this is a forward slash (/). Backward slashes (\) are used for internal file names and in programming, but do not accidentally use them in web addresses. You will receive an error message if you do.

☞   ALSO KNOWN AS   ☜
sapling: young greyhound

Answer 31   (B) dilatory
[L. *dilatus*, postponed; delayed]

He was so dilatory in his work habits that we considered firing him.

Q. You have said that every paragraph must have a single, controlling idea. But that can be expressed in one sentence. Where does the rest of the paragraph come from?

A. It comes as support and follow-up for the main idea. The limited idea can be developed by using any of several patterns.

- EXAMPLES You may use a series of examples or one extended example.
  Ask: like what/whom?
  Do: use familiar things.
  Don't: use irrelevant examples.

- DESCRIPTION Decide ahead of time the dominant impression you wish to make.
  Ask: what does it look/sound/taste/feel/smell like?
  Do: use concrete details.
  Don't: use vague, abstract words or simply tell instead of showing.

- CLASSIFICATION All parts should be equally important and the method consistent.
  Ask: what parts or divisions does it have?
  Do: research before writing.
  Don't: give a mere listing with no strong purpose.

- NARRATION You are telling a story. Choose only details that move it along.
  Ask: what happened?
  Do: relive the incident in your imagination.
  Don't: have an unclear or jumbled sense of time and events.

- COMPARISON/CONTRAST Present each whole separately or alternate from point to point.

Ask: how are they alike or different?
Do: balance each item with its counterpart.
Don't: stack the deck or use irrelevant similarities/differences.

- DEFINITION   Place it in a category and then distinguish it from others in that category.
Ask: what is it or what does it mean?
Do: use precise words as simply as possible.
Don't: skip necessary elements or include unnecessary details.

- PROCESS   Also called how-to, it depends on a clear step-by-step description.
Ask: how do I do it or how does it work?
Do: use firsthand knowledge or thorough research.
Don't: fail to break the process into small, sequential steps.

- CAUSE/EFFECT   Cause focuses on reasons; effect focuses on results.
Ask: why, or what happened as a result?
Do: resist bias and be thoroughly analytical.
Don't: give weak or remote reasons.

Q. Which is correct: "Neither of them are right" or "Neither of them is right"?

A. Keep this hint in mind: the subject controls its verb, and intervening phrases don't usually change that. The confusing element in this example is the prepositional phrase *of them*, which separates the subject from its verb. The subject is the word *neither*. It is singular because it means not this one or that one. So it needs a singular verb — *is*. Other pronouns that are relentlessly singular include *either, each*, and pronouns ending in *-one, -body*, and *-thing*.

Q. I notice that you ask listeners to call in assigned figures of speech each week. I can usually think of some, but my question is, why do we even use them?

A. Broadly speaking, there are two levels of language: literal language, which treats words and phrases in their strict, unadorned sense, and figurative language, which is symbolic and creative. I think it's in human nature to adorn, to imagine, to soar, to slip the surly bonds of literalness. Figures of speech add verve and poetry to life. They tickle the imagination and encourage creative juices to flow. And when one tries to track down the origin of a particular figure of speech, there are historical and sociological bonuses. Added to all this is the fact that figurative language has been around for over a thousand years. Greek drama gave us a storehouse of figures that are useful to this day: simile, metaphor, hyperbole, metonymy, and a host of others. If you want to be overwhelmed by the complexity of it all, visit Dr. Gideon Burton's *Forest of Rhetoric* by using this URL: http://humanities.byu.edu/rhetoric/silva.htm Meanwhile, how many figures of speech can you think of that contain the word red (as in *caught red-handed*)?

Q. I gather that a Tom Swifty is some kind of pun, but I don't quite get the idea.

A. Tom Swift appears in a series of novels written for boys by Victor Appleton, who used a clunky verb/adverb pattern for tag lines (*Tom said sadly; Tom said quietly*), something that invites ridicule and satire. So it's a pun with a pattern as these examples will attest:

- "Wouldn't you prefer a poodle?" asked her father doggedly.
- "Finally, I'm an actor!" Tom said playfully.
- "Fire!" yelled Tom alarmingly.
- "It's between my sole and my heel," said Tom archly.
- "I dropped the toothpaste," signaled Tom, crest-fallen.
- "Don't try to pull the wool over my eyes," Tom said sheepishly.
- "I'm as strong as a sled dog," Tom said huskily.

To the masochists among us: simply enter "tom swifties" into your favorite search engine and you'll be able to savor thousands more.

☞   WORD FACT   ☜

There is a 7- letter word that contains 10 words without rearranging any of its letters: THEREIN: the, there, he, in, rein, her, here, ere, herein, therein.

Answer 32   (C) convincing
[L. *cogere*, to force]

His argument was so cogent that even his opponents turned into believers.

Q. I am always annoyed by Corporate America's refusal to stand up and use the word *fired*. Do they really think that *downsizing* and *involuntary separation* are going to fool anyone or make the fired employee feel better?

A. Agreed. The euphemisms fly almost as fast as they do in the presence of death. We encounter *planned turnovers*, though that may have been the last thing the <u>worker</u> was planning. *You won't be moving forward with the company, Smedley; you've been culled.*

The prefix *de-*(away from) gets a workout. Employees get to experience *decruitment, dehiring, deinstallation, deselection,* and *destaffing.* As you're escorted to the plant exit, you may hear talk of *uninstallation, rightsizing, vocational adjustment,* and *redeployment.* Sorry about that; we had to transition you to effect a work force imbalance correction.

Q. Fox News had this: "Officials are trying to staunch the flow of terrorists into our country." I think that's incorrect word use.

A. And I think you're correct; it should be stanch. Use stanch as a verb, meaning to stop the flow, as in *The surgeon tried to stanch the hemorrhage*. Use staunch as an adjective, as in *She is a staunch supporter of anti-drug laws*.

Q. Which is preferable, *different from* or *different than*?

A. *Different from* is more common. *Different to* seems to be preferred in Britain.

Different than is generally used when a clause follows the word than: *Today, things are different than they used to be.* This could also be rendered as, *Today, things are different from what they used to be.*

Q. Are you familiar with the term aleatory art?

A. I did know that aleatory referred to gambling; it comes from the Latin word *alea*, chance or a die. Your question reminded me that there are creative people— musicians and authors and artists—who make chance an integral part of what they create. Some aleatory practitioners program computers to generate random poems or notes of music. Others allow the audience or readership to choose alternate versions. For instance, Julio Cortazar's novel *Hopscotch* contained expendable chapters and alternate chapter reading suggestions. B.S. Johnson's novel *The Unfortunates* consisted of a box of separately bound chapters that the reader could rearrange on a whim. Aleatory writing seems to be an important symbol of postmodernism, and the *ucla hypermedia studio* is working on " the integration of aleatory real-time animation into works of dramatic fiction."

Q. I have a question concerning the correct way to write the plural form of acronyms, numbers, and some abbreviations. Should there be an apostrophe before the s?

A. A few years back, the answer would have been to use the apostrophe. Now, the style seems to be to avoid it unless confusion would result. So you will encounter CEOs, a number of 4s, and the 1990s. But in abbreviations containing more than one period, use the apostrophe to form plurals: M.A.'s and Ph.D.'s. And you'll want to add the apostrophe when dealing with letters: dot your i's and cross your t's and mind your p's and q's. By the way, you won't be *wrong* if you use the apostrophe all the time for acronyms and the like; you'll just be unfashionable.

QUICK QUIZ
33. the indentation on the bottom of a champagne or wine bottle:

(A) punt   (B) duff   (C) frass   (D) jess

Q. Why do some words in the dictionary have raised numbers? Two examples are forte[1] and truck[2].

A. Those raised numbers are called superscripts, and they are used with words that have identical spellings but come from totally different sources. For instance, you'll find pedo-[1] and pedo-[2] listed as prefixes. The first comes from a Greek word meaning soil; the latter comes from a Greek word meaning child. And even though children are notorious for getting dirty, the identical spellings are a sheer accident of history.

Q. I heard a newscaster speak of a school *closure* due to snow. Shouldn't that be *closing*?

A. Good call on your part. Closure can have two meanings:
> (1) condition of being closed up—*closure of the eyelids; closure of an incision.* Generally, save this use for medical contexts.
> (2) completion of a situation— *looking for closure on the divorce.*
> Closing, the word that he or she should have used, means a shutting down or sealing—*a school closing; a road closing.* By the way, closure the door on your way out.

Q. While watching a rerun of *Star Trek: Voyager,* I heard Security Officer Tuvok ask a crewmate to participate in an interrogation because, "You may be able to help me evaluate the verisimilitude of his answers." Is that correct?

A. As you went on to say in your note, verisimilitude means giving the *appearance* of truth; it could actually be a carefully crafted lie. Tuvok was known for his stilted vocabulary, but he should have used *veracity* instead. For ordinary mortals, there's nothing wrong with the word *truth.*

Q. There are some words that we read, but never hear. This led me into trouble last week when I used the word *placebo* in class and was corrected for pronouncing it *place'-bow.*

A. I'm no stranger to that phenomenon. I remember being embarrassed in grammar school to discover that *omit* did not rhyme with *vomit.* At any rate, you discovered that it is pronounced plah-see'-bow, and I'm sure that you knew it referred to a deliberately useless medicine or procedure designed to enhance a patient's expectation. Placebos are often used in drug trials to separate truly efficacious medicines from a user's optimism. It comes from the Latin *placebo,* I shall please. Equally interesting is a word invented to describe the opposite effect: *nocebo.* In Latin, this means I shall harm, and it describes the effect of a patient's negative expectations on his or her health. There are ethical considerations in making patients believe that a harmless substance is going to make them ill, but tests have been conducted on bronchitis and allergy sufferers, and the results confirm that negative expectations play as large a role as positive expectations.

Q. What does the term "financially esculent" mean?

A. This one led me to many dead ends, so I tossed the question to my son (Mike, Jr.) who works for *Money Magazine.* Here's what he came up with when he asked around the editorial offices of AOL Time-Life:

Answer 33   (A) punt
[Fr. *pointe*, point]

The punt is designed to add strength to a wine bottle.

- Carol Gwinn, Copy Chief, *Fortune Magazine*: " I've never even heard of 'esculent.' Who is this guy?"
- Pat Feimster, Copy Chief, *Money Magazine*: "I couldn't find esculent in any of my financial dictionaries."
- Jason Zweig, Senior Writer / Columnist, *Money Magazine*: "Your dad wanted to know if *financially esculent* had more than a metaphorical sense. Can't imagine that it would. A 'financially esculent' company could only be one with a tasty balance sheet or a savory income statement..."
- Carol Loomis, Editor-at-Large, *Fortune Magazine*: "So what do we think about *financially esculent*? I'm like your father: groping. But maybe it means something that throws off money, such as a dividend-paying stock. Sorry to be of so little help. But thanks for introducing me to a new word. And introducing Warren Buffett, too. I asked him if he'd ever heard the word, and he hadn't."

How's that for a first-class research staff?

Q. This appeared in my local newspaper; read it and weep. "The bones are individually sealed with wax over red chord and authenticated by a church authority."

A. **sniffle** Say, if the church organ was playing in the background, there may have been chords wafting about. The writer should have used the spelling *cord* to describe heavy string used as a binding. Use chord for harmonized sounds, for a line segment that joins two points on a curve, or for an emotional response (*his sermon struck a sympathetic chord in the congregation*). And if those bones had been hollowed out, I suppose we could say they were cored.

Q. A news item reported that some convicted financial officers look forward to their release and "the possibility of becoming respectful again." Something's wrong with that sentence.

A. As wrong as a $3 bill. Respectful means *showing* respect; it is directed outward toward other people. These miscreants want to have their reputations rehabilitated so they can once again *receive* esteem and be respectable; it is self-centered. And don't throw the word respective into the mix. It means particular or separate, as in *They returned to their respective jail cells*.

Q. For your collection of misused and abused words:

- a CNN reporter observed that, "We're all sitting on a tight hair trigger."
- an MSNBC screen crawler advised us that, "The vice is closing around Saddam Hussein."
- a caption under a photo of a GI working on a Humvee explained that he was attaching a wench to the vehicle.

A. Great—you actually saw what was there instead of filling in for journalistic sins! Hair trigger refers to a gun trigger adjusted so that it responds to very slight pressure, so a "tight" hair trigger cancels everything out and ruins the image. And *sitting* on a hair trigger? Talk about a mixed metaphor, not to mention uncomfortable.... The image used with

---

QUICK QUIZ
34. plangent:
(A) bright in color (B) spherical
(C) loud & reverberating (D) vegetating

Saddam is a reference to the clamping and squeezing device known as a vise; save vice for industrial-strength sin. Speaking of which, the Vice Squad will be coming after that GI and his hapless girlfriend, the wench. That is, unless he was attaching a winch to the Hummer for power hoisting and hauling. Keep them coming, folks; they're great.

Q.　　Should it be "Choose whoever you want" or "Choose whomever you want"?

A.　　To answer, let me contrast two sentences:
　　　　Choose whomever you want.
　　　　Choose whoever raises her hand first.
In both cases, the following clause acts as the direct object of the verb *choose*, so we can't use that as the basis of choice. Always examine what a word is doing in <u>its own</u> clause.

　　　In "Choose whomever you want," *whomever* is the direct
　　　　object of *want*.
　　　In "Choose whoever raises her hand first," *whoever* is
　　　　the subject of *raises*.
　　　Whoever = subject spelling; whomever = object spell-
　　　　ing.
Here's a related example: (AP) "But those involved in what is known as 'site exploitation' aren't interviewing the hundreds of Iraqi scientists *whom* U.S. officials have said would be the key to finding any banned weapons." Here, *who* is needed as the subject of *would be*.

Q.　　This exchange appeared in a nationally syndicated column. The question was, "Someone who dislikes all people is a 'misanthrope.' Someone who dislikes all women is a 'misogynist.' What's someone who dislikes all men?" The answer was, "If you don't count manhater, there's no word for that."

A.   The correct answer is that there *is* a word for that. Misandry means a hatred of men; the practitioner would be a misandrist. We have to be careful about miseducating people when it comes to language.

Q.   What do you make of this sentence, which appeared in last Sunday's paper? "Grouped together under the title 'Historic Driving Journeys,' the peregrinations are divided into five areas."

A.   While the writer seems to have wanted to avoid repeating the word *journey*, the word is a bit pretentious for its context—an article about family travel presented in a general circulation newspaper. *Trips* would have done the job. [It came from the Latin *peregrinus*—foreign, wandering, migratory. In turn, that was a blend of *per*, through, and *ager*, land].

Q.   From a recent Letter to the Editor: "If the mayor isn't satisfied with the current level of cooperation between departments, she should change course and try a new tact."

A.   I see what you mean: tact was used where tack should have been. Tact is a sensitivity that respects the feelings of others. Tack is a term borrowed from sailing, where a ship turns into the wind in order to change direction. The metaphorical meaning here is to change one's course of action. Of course, if the mayor's old style was to ride roughshod over everyone's feelings, the opposite would be a new tact.

Answer 34   (C) loud & reverberating
[L. *plangere*, to strike or lament]

The organ had a plangent sound that stirred the congregation.

Q.   My mother-in-law posed this question the other day, and we were all at a loss. Then I realized, I know just the person to ask! What is the origin of the phrase "naked as a jay bird?"

A.   You pose an interesting question, particularly because most experts don't have a secure answer. The real puzzle, of course, is that far from being naked, the bluejay is covered with brilliant blue and white and black feathers—a veritable riot of clothing.

Evan Morris (*The Word Detective*) and Christine Ammer (*Cool Cats, Top Dogs, and Other Beastly Expressions*) are two wordsmiths who at least tried to formulate an answer. Their speculations:

1. In 19th century America, jay was slang for a hick, a simpleton, a gullible person. In that case, naked as a jay would refer to a completely vulnerable person, not to a bird.

2. All perching birds, including jays, are born with hardly any down at all, making them quite helpless.

So "naked" turns out to be the easy part, expressing vulnerability. "Jay" is the problem. Human or bird? Take your pick. No one seems to know.

Q.   Where did "ollie ollie oxen free" come from? For that matter, exactly what does it mean?

A.   As you went on to mention, it is used when children play Hide and Go Seek.

It probably started out as "All-ee, all-ee, outs in free," a call from the person who was "it" letting those hidden (the outs) know it was safe to come in. The -*ee* was added for emphasis and for its piercing quality; I remember sitting on my bike outside a friend's house and hollering, "Oh, Ralphieeee!" at the top of my lungs when I was young.

There are many regional variations, most of them from dialectical interference. It reminds me of the old parlor game, Telephone. Variations include Ollie Ollie in come free, Oly Oly oxen free, Ollie Ollie oxenfreed, Alley Alley oats in free, Oly Oly ocean free, All-ye All-ye outs in free, and in Minnesota, Oly Oly Olsen's free. Check with Lena.

Q.   I found this in a local newspaper: "While sorting through the maize of media available in the area for your advertising message, we suggest that you take into consideration the population you want to reach."

A.   Sounds corny to me. What was meant was maze, a labyrinth. Maze comes from an Old English word meaning to bewilder. The word incorrectly used, maize, means corn. It also shows up as a color adjective, as in maize and blue.

Q.   I'm a retired park ranger, and some spelling has been puzzling me for years. Should we write campfire wood, camp firewood, or camp fire wood? I saw all three during my career.

A.   It's going to be one of the first two compounds, and logic—rather than grammar—will solve it. Are you buying wood for the entire camp (camp firewood) or wood for your own campfire (campfire wood)? I think the latter fits the reality. In a similar vein, the youth organization used to

---

QUICK QUIZ
35. accolent

(A) important (B) satisfactory (C) distant (D) neighboring

be called Camp Fire Girls. When boys were admitted in 1975, the spelling changed to Campfire Boys and Girls.

Q. I forgot the word that means loss of compass direction, i.e., coming off a cloverleaf on the freeway and not knowing in which direction you're going. I know the word is not vertigo. Can you help?

A. I suggested the word disorientation, but the gentleman didn't think that was it, either. I never heard back from the listener, so I wasn't able to get an initial letter to help narrow the search. I did contact the Alzheimer's Disease Education and Referral (ADEAR) Center and received this answer: "We could not find a medical term for loss of sense of direction. Etiology suggests that disorientation is the most appropriate term." Any suggestions out there?

Q. The word factoid—does it mean a brief, interesting fact or does it mean an outright fabrication? I've seen both.

A. Originally, it meant a spurious fact. It was invented by Norman Mailer and used in his 1973 book *Marilyn*. As he defined them, factoids are "facts which have no existence before appearing in a magazine or newspaper, creations which are not so much lies as a product to manipulate emotion in the Silent Majority." In recent years (probably due to magazines and TV news programs) stats and trivia dropped in as fillers have been referred to as factoids.

Q. Is it *in concert with* or *in consort with*?

A. I would have sworn that *in concert with,* meaning in cooperation with someone, was the correct choice. In fact, it's the one that shows up in Richard Spears' *American Idioms*

Dictionary and in *Cassell's Dictionary of English Idioms*. But I was thrown for a loop by the 4th edition of *The American Heritage Dictionary*, which gives this as the 4th noun definition of **consort**: Partnership; association: *governed in consort with her advisers*. Under **concert**, The AHD gives this example of unity: *acted in concert on the issue*. *The Oxford English Dictionary* cites a 1712 entry for *in concert with* and a 1634 entry for *in consort with*. It would seem, therefore, that both are acceptable. Previously, the cliché with *consort* in it that I was familiar with was the police blotter's *he is known to consort with criminals*. Google displays a paltry 6,320 hits for *in consort with* and 909,000 hits for *in concert with*, so that says much about frequency of use.

Q. What do you call it when words are repeated in a sentence, but as different parts of speech, such as verb/noun? I'm thinking of examples such as *walk the walk, talk the talk*, and *name names*.

A. This is known as polyptoton, which is defined as repetition of the same word or root in different grammatical functions or forms. It comes from Gk. *poly*, "many" and *ptotos*, "falling" or *ptosis*, "[grammatical] case".

Q. Where did the use of the word "some" come from in modifying the number of something? As in "There were some 100 people at the meeting last night." I can understand if there were "some 25,000 balloons released," but it is also

---

Answer 35 (D) neighboring
[L. *accolare*, to dwell near]

In a rain forest, accolent plants often
develop symbiotic relationships.

---

used with very small numbers that a reporter should be able to count accurately.

A. It does seem a bit lazy when fewer items are involved, doesn't it? Yet *The American Heritage Dictionary*, 4th edition, gives as much legitimacy to "some" when used to mean a small number of unspecified objects as it does to "some" meaning indefinite or approximate when applied to a large (almost uncountable) number.

The Oxford English Dictionary, 1st edition, was a bit stricter. It defined this use of some as "an indefinite or unspecified (but not large) number of persons or animals." To James Murray, size did matter, but in a direction opposite to your position.

The old *Funk & Wagnalls* used "estimated" as a synonym: "Some 80 people attended the meeting."

Q. I've seen a number of crazy boat names this summer that I'd like to share with your listeners. They include Moby Deck, Codfather, Tooth Ferry, Pier Pressure, and Knot On Call.

A. Those are funny. Obviously, a lot of imagination goes into creating these things. Here are a few more: Guppy Love, A Knotty Buoy, Passing Wind, Berth Control, Just Add Water, Out To Launch, Sea Nile, and Salesman Ship.

Q. Is the word "losingest" (referring to the Detroit Tigers) proper?

A. Are you kidding? Haven't you checked their record? Seriously, it's an awkward creation, but I've seen it even in newspapers. It's not proper in the sense that you'd want to use it in a formal situation, but it is an acknowledged slang term.

The American Heritage Dictionary, 4th Edition, lists it as such. Entering "losingest" in Google returns 1,650 hits, so it's out there.

Q.   Could you discuss on your show with Ron how some of these plurals came into being? (1) a murder of crows; (2) a mob of kangaroos; (3) a cry of players/actors; (4) a parliament of owls; (5) a pencil of lines

A.   Those inventive plurals are called collective nouns. Some of them are used by ordinary people and even by professionals in the field, such as zoologists; herd and flock are two of the most common. Most of them, however, were deliberately made up, either to imitate a sound or to mirror a behavior. They are seldom used in ordinary conversation and never in scientific journals. Who made them up? Writers, poets, jokesters, punsters, and just about anybody with a pen.

What they are all about is fun, and there have been several books written about them. One that comes to mind is *An Exaltation of Larks* by James Lipton. Also, take a look at http://www.askoxford.com/askttheexperts/collective/. The *Ask Oxford* site has so many animal collectives listed that you have to click through in alphabetical order.

☞   BUMPER STICKER   ☜
When you've seen one shopping center you've seen a mall.

QUICK QUIZ
36. Which word means "to criticize severely"?

(A) colligate   (B) profligate   (C) castigate (D) mitigate

Q.   I used the term "easy as pie" the other day and a friend stopped me and said, "Come on, now. Making a pie is NOT easy!" So where did that saying originate?

A.   I agree; baking a pie isn't the easiest thing in the world. But the phrase refers to <u>eating</u> pie, not baking it. We use a related phrase when we say, *that's a piece of cake.*

Q.   I was wondering about the word "stat" that doctors use for hospital emergencies. The dictionary definition is "a clipped form of statistic." Is that the origin of the word?

A.   The "stat" in medical circles comes from the Latin word *statim*, an adverb that meant *at once* or *instantly*. As it turns out, the medical "stat" has no connection with the word statistics. That word ultimately came from a Latin word that meant position or form of government. State and statute share the root with statistics. If you look at your dictionary again, you'll find stat[1] and stat[2].

Q.   How did punctuation ever get started?

A.   In our era, primarily because monks began to mark up scripture for public readings. Spacing, slash marks, and parentheses probably showed up first. We take punctuation for granted in our day, but to see what writing used to look like, revise a paragraph by eliminating every single mark. You'll quickly discover how much we depend on punctuation to help us divide thoughts into grammatical units so we can understand more readily. Various punctuation marks also clue us in on intonation and rhythm and stress, all useful in expressing emotion, emphasis, or asides. They also enhance contrasts and make connections more obvious. That's the point of punctuation.

Q. I couldn't believe it when I caught this in a news article: "The protest disbursed quickly when the police arrived."

A. Ouch! To disburse means *to pay out* or *expend*. The verb needed was disperse – *to scatter* or *disband*.

Q. I was startled to read that English has no future tense. What's that all about?

A. Technically, that's true. As far as built-in tense endings, we have a present tense (*I see, I want*) and a past tense (*I saw, I wanted*). Every other time variation, including the future, depends on auxiliaries. To express the future, we add auxiliary verbs to the present-tense or present-participle spelling: *shall, will, be going to, be about to*. We also use future adverbs, such as *tomorrow* and *soon*. So even though we don't have dedicated, built-in future endings, we all still have a future.

Q. Why do plural spellings have to be so difficult? Why can't we just slap an –*s* on the back of every noun to signify more than one?

A. I sympathize with that one, but remember that most nouns do exactly that. Irregular noun plurals occur only in a few hundred words, though they tend to attract more than their share of attention. As for the cause of irregular

---

Answer 36
(C) castigate [L. *castigare*, to beat]

The boss castigated the marketing manager in front of the whole staff.

nouns, we have to blame history and country of origin. For instance, seven nouns from Old English or Germanic change their vowels to express the plural: man/men, woman/women, louse/lice, tooth/teeth, goose/geese, mouse/mice, and foot/feet. Some add *–en*, such as children, oxen, and brethren. A few change an *–f* to a *–v*, as in wives, loaves, and halves. Some plurals sit on the fence and have two forms, among them scarfs/scarves, dwarfs/dwarves, and fish/fishes. This also happens when some words come straight from Latin (focuses or foci, indexes or indices) or from Greek (criterions or criteria, automatons or automata). The real jokers, of course, make no changes at all: deer/deer, sheep/sheep, series/series.

Q.   The phrase *to turn a blind eye on something*—where did that come from?

A.   Finally, a phrase origin question that has a definite answer! There is unanimous agreement that this phrase, meaning to deliberately overlook or ignore, goes back to the siege of Copenhagen in 1801. Lord Horatio Nelson was ordered to withdraw from naval engagement, but he pretended not to notice the signals being given by the flagship. He did this by placing his spy glass over the eye that had been blinded in an earlier battle and declaring to his officers that he saw no signal whatsoever. He achieved a major victory by ignoring orders.

Q.   I get confused by abbreviations such as *i.e., e.g.,* and *viz.* Can you help?

A.   These abbreviations are easier to remember if you know a little Latin. The abbreviation i.e. stands for *id est,* which means "that is." (CW *is the abbreviation for continuous wave —i.e., non-pulsed source of electromagnetic radiation.*) *Exempli gratia* is the source for e.g., and it means "for the sake of example." It is always followed, logically enough, by examples. (*This section of the zoo houses canids, e.g., foxes, wolves, jackals, and coyotes.*) Viz. is the abbreviation for *videlicet*, which means "namely." (*The three lawyers — viz. Allen, Rivera, and Smith — are now in the court room.*) The abbreviation et al comes from *et alii*, "and others." (*Elizabethan playwrights – Shakespeare et al – delighted in word play.*) Finally, since etc. stands for *et cetera*, "and others," never write *and etc.*

Q. When is it proper to use persons or people?

A. In fussier days of yore, people was considered a general term (*Hundreds of people had gathered in the high school auditorium*), and persons was saved for small, specific numbers (*Three persons had special passes.*) These days, persons sounds a bit stiff, perhaps because of its use in phrases such as *person or persons unknown*. Stay with *a person* and two *people* or more.

Q. My mother says that the Arctic got its name from a Latin word that meant bear, because there are polar bears there. And because there are <u>no</u> polar bears at the southern pole, it was named Antarctica (anti-) to show the absence of bears.

A. There are two parallel realities going on here, but they are not coterminal. The Australian Antarctic Division confirms that there are polar bears in the Arctic and none in

---

QUICK QUIZ
37. esculent:

(A) overheated   (B) educated   (C) bent over (D) edible

---

the Antarctic, but that's not how the continents were named. The ancient Greeks knew about the Arctic and named it after the northern constellation—Makros Arktos (or Ursa Major, as we know it from the Latin), translated as Great Bear in English. The Greeks were big fans of symmetry, so sight unseen, they decided that there must be a similar cold land mass at the opposite pole: AntArktos, or opposite the bear.

Q. Which is correct: unrelated or nonrelated? I have encountered both.

A. Sometimes the meanings of *non-* and *un-* are quite distinct. For instance, a nonprofit organization is not supposed to turn a profit; if it does, it breaks the law. On the other hand, a business that is unprofitable is supposed to reap profits, so it's in trouble. Likewise, a nonscheduled airline operates without a regular schedule of flights; it runs charters. But an unscheduled landing implies that there is a normal schedule that has been altered because of an emergency. But this does not seem to apply to unrelated and nonrelated, which are treated as synonyms in sample documents, such as the Minnesota Code of Law (*"A guardian may be related or unrelated to the child. A child living with a nonrelated legal guardian shall be eligible for foster care..."*) and the Bureau of Labor Statistics (*"Unrelated individuals. These are persons who are not living with any relatives. Such individuals may live alone, reside in a nonrelated family household, or live in group quarters with other unrelated individuals.*) In practice, the words seem to be interchangeable.

Q. I grew up in Richmond, Indiana; thus I may have been exposed to some Hoosier or ethnic German vocabulary that is widely unknown . The word "scoch" (my guess at spelling) means a tad, a wee bit, a small amount, and a smidgen. My Microsoft "Word" program's thesaurus doesn't offer a clue as to correct spelling when I look up bit, tad, and smidgen. An example of my use of the word: "The soup needs a SCOCH more salt." Have you heard of this word?

A.   In fact, skosh is a word that my confederates and I used in the 1950s in Chicago. *The American Heritage Dictionary,* 4th edition, designates it as slang and says that it comes from the Japanese sukoshi. It doesn't define sukoshi, but we may deduce that it means tad or smidgen. I found an online diary written by a WWII P.O.W. which says that his Japanese captors always used the phrase *sukoshi matte,* meaning a short time, when asked about the end of captivity.

Q.   Where did the phrase *in and of itself* come from?

A.   I was not able to track down its history in the English language, but I did check on its Latin precedents. It's a combination of two short phrases that were quite important in medieval philosophy. *In se,* translated as "in itself," meant essential, having its own essence—something that does not depend on anything else for being. A tree, for instance, is something in itself, whereas its color, height, and so on couldn't exist without that essence of treeness. *Per se,* translated as "of itself," is something known by itself—not the product of proof. For instance, philosophy can be known by itself, by the unaided labors of the mind, whereas theology is the product of faith. So when we speak of something *in and of itself,* we point to its very essence and to the fact that we don't need any external references.

Answer 37 (D) edible
[L. *esca*, food]

The morel is an esculent mushroom.

Q. I often hear the phrase *to grouse,* meaning to complain or grumble. What does that have to do with the game bird? Does it chatter a lot?

A. As far as I can tell, the "complain" meaning of the word has nothing to do with the bird, even though they are identical in spelling. Many authorities say that the origin of *to grouse* is unknown, but a few point to the Old French verb *grousser,* to murmur. That sounds reasonable.

Q. When people reach for a simile to describe a really dumb person, they tend to pick on animals. Why is that?

A. It's true that we use dumb bunny, dumb as an ox, dodo, dumb as a slug, harebrain, dumb as a Junebug, dumb as a carp, dumb as a dead moose, dumb as a jackass, birdbrain, and featherbrain, but it doesn't stop there.

Think of all the inanimate objects that show up in similes: dumb as a sack of doorknobs, dumb as a bag of nails, dumb as a sack of hammers, dumb as a box of rocks, dumb as a box of hair, and dumb as a sack of excrement; dumb as a brick, dumb as a post, dumb as a tree stump, dumb as a box of dirt, dumb as a doorstop, dumb as a stop sign, dumb as a doornail, and dumb as a mud fence; dumb as a stick, dumb as a wooden bucket, dumb as a pair of cleats, dumb as a divot, dumb as a wedge, dumb as a 2x4, dumb as a mudflap, dumb as a lampshade, dumb as a stale chunk of meatloaf, dumb as a wall, dumb as a shoelace, dumb as a diaper, dumb as a rope, and dumb as a ball of clay. Enough dumb to make you numb.

Q. I can't help but cringe every time I hear someone use the phrase "Native American" when they actually mean "American Indian." I am a Native American as I was born in America. That would include everyone from Canada to Argentina, as far as I can figure. Please comment on this, and, if

I am wrong in some way about this, please explain where I might be "native" to, since I was born in North America, as well as all parents on both respective sides of the family tree for about the last 300 years.

A.   Group names are always a thorny issue, especially if you're not a member of the group. The word *native*, of course, comes from a Latin word meaning *born in*, so as you mention, <u>anyone</u> who is not an immigrant is a native. And beyond that, I am old enough to remember when *native* had pejorative connotations. It was a term used by superior folks who could afford to look down on primitives, savages, wild men. When Jungle Jim said, "The natives are restless tonight," he wasn't being sympathetic about their insomnia. And to the British Empire, *going native* was about the worst fate that could befall a gentleman and officer of a regiment. You simply didn't trade in your red blazer for a loincloth. On the other hand, using the word *Indian* perpetuates bad geography, since Columbus thought he had reached India, but I notice that many tribes still use the word. I think the term *Proto-American* has merit, because the inhabitants that Columbus encountered preceded any Europeans, but I recognize that it sounds like something out of an anthropology textbook, on the same lines as *Indigenous American*. The great irony here is that in prehistoric times, people from Asia crossed the then-existent land bridge to enter this continent. We're ALL visitors.

QUICK QUIZ
38. abulia means the inability to

(A) make decisions (B) sleep (C) remember things (D) eat

Q.   I know that a nerd is a socially inept person, usually a technically-oriented person, but what's the origin of the word? It doesn't sound like Greek or Latin to me.

A.   You are correct: a nerd is an uninteresting, hyper-focused technical geek. Now, computer users are forever being admonished to read the manuals that come with software and hardware before attempting to use them. But there are people who seem to know these things instinctively without consulting the instructions. Their motto is, **N**ot **E**veryone **R**eads **D**irections. Hence the word *nerd*.

If you have stayed with this answer, I can now reveal that the previous paragraph is pure hogwash. I've always wanted to start a phony folk etymology myself. The actual source seems to be a character in Dr. Seuss' *If I Ran the Zoo*. His Nerd was a comically obnoxious creature.

Q.   Should it be a cyclic pattern of weather changes or a cyclical pattern of weather changes?

A.   *The American Heritage Dictionary*, 4th Edition, regards either as correct, though *cyclic* appears more frequently as a scientific term in chemistry, botany, math, and so on. But in common use, we'd speak of a *cyclical theory of history*, for example. My guess is that euphony is a factor in making the choice.

Q.   I'm looking for a word to describe a person who flaunts his education.

A.   Try one of these: arrogant, conceited, condescending, egotistical, haughty, narcissistic, ostentatious, overbearing, patronizing, pedantic, pretentious, pompous, self-important , snobbish, stuck-up, supercilious, vain, whiz kid.

Q. Should it be *inundated by* or *inundated with*?

A. Both are used. For instance, we find these examples in dictionaries: "...was inundated by calls, telegrams, and letters." Marya Mannes (*Webster's Third New International Dictionary*, unabridged); "The theater was inundated with requests for tickets." (*American Heritage Dictionary*, 4th Edition); "The whole system is inundated with the tides of joy." Ralph Waldo Emerson (*Century Dictionary & Cyclopedia*). If you choose to go with popularity, Google has 27,200 instances of *inundated by* and 80,500 instances of *inundated with*.

Q. If a sentence ends with an abbreviation, is a second period needed to end the sentence?

A. No. In such an instance, a single period does double duty: it serves the abbreviation and it ends the sentence simultaneously. *I'll meet you at 4:00 p.m.* The only time you'll see more than one period at a time is in an ellipsis, where multiple periods signal an omission of words. *The person in charge... fled the country as investigators closed in.* The rule is this: use three periods to signify an omission within a sentence; if the omission comes at the end of a sentence, add a fourth period as end punctuation.

☞ THE GAME OF THE NAME ☜
Charles came from a Germanic word meaning man.

Answer 38   (A) make decisions
[Gr. *boule*, will]

Abulia is often expressed as inability to make
decisions or set goals.

Q. My wife and I disagree on the spelling of the word *baited*, as in, *"He stood there with baited breath."* I say it's like the action of a hunter where he suppresses his breath to avoid startling his prey or ruining a shot, so it should be spelled B-A-I-T. She says I spend too much time in the woods.

A. Scramble back into your blind, guy. The word has nothing to do with bait, as in hunting or fishing. The correct spelling is bated. It's an old word that means suspended, so your mention of suppressing a breath was on target. It is related to the verb *abate*, as in *"We waited until the storm abated,"* and to the legal and tax term *abatement*.

Q. I was standing in line waiting to pay for a round of golf, and I overheard a guy at the counter explaining that the number displayed at the first tee would tell each golfer where the flag was placed for that day. All he or she had to do was look at the diagram displayed on the cart for each hole's green. As he explained it, "Each green is divided into quadrants — 1, 2, 3, 4, and 5." I thought quadrant meant four, not five.

A. You are right, sir. Don't let that counter man keep score for you. When five divisions are involved, we have two words at our disposal. Quintile comes from the Latin (as does quadrant), and pentad comes from the Greek.

Q. To give someone the cold shoulder—where does that come from?

A. There are differences of opinion on this one. The folk etymology version says that in the Middle Ages, unwelcome guests were given a cold shoulder of meat rather than a hot meal. But a meal with meat (even cold meat) was a luxury that most people seldom enjoyed; it wasn't punishment. For another, it doesn't show up in print until 1816, when it appears in Sir Walter Scott's novel,

The Antiquary. Not only does this late date eliminate a medieval source, but Scott uses it in the sense of a dismissive shrug of the shoulder, not a cold meal. No shoulder to cry on here.

Q.   Aside from the potty mouths among us, I notice that people often go out of the way to avoid swearing, instead saying Jeepers Creepers, cripes, darn it, gosh, and so on. Is there a name for this substitution?

A.   The attempt to circumvent taking the name of the Lord in vain is often referred to as a minced oath. Mince can mean chopping food into fine pieces, but in this sense it means to restrain or to euphemize. Even so, some churches do not take kindly to the practice. One ecclesiastical web site warns, "... a little thought will lead anyone to the conclusion that 'gosh' is not an appropriate word for a Christian to use on any occasion whatsoever."

Q.   I found this in the paper: "Most of the wood used to build the home is local," said architect [*name withheld*] of Chicago, "from the predominate ash to the cedar ceiling beams and columns of Douglas fir."

A.   Not a common mistake, and probably one founded on pronunciation or hearing. Predominate is the verb form: *People hope that good will predominate over evil.* The adjective form was needed here, and that is spelled predominant.

QUICK QUIZ
39. Which word means unyielding or inflexible?

(A) adamantine (B) levantine (C) elephantine (D) legantine

Q.   Could you discuss affect and effect?

A.   These two bedevil many people. The trick is to pay attention to parts of speech, not always a pleasant task. Here's a rundown.

AFFECT:

> **Noun:** feeling or emotion (used mostly by psychologists)
>> *The patient's face showed no affect at all.*
>
> **Verb**: to have an influence on (substitute "change" to check)
>> *Inflation can affect the buying power of the dollar.*
>>
>> *Rheumatic fever can affect the heart.*

EFFECT:

> **Noun**: something brought about by a cause (it always comes second)
>> *Addicts have to increase the dose to have a steady effect.*
>
> power to produce an outcome (substitute "result" to check)
>> *The news had an immediate effect on my family.*
>
> **Verb:**   to bring into existence or to produce (substitute "create" to check)
>> *Specific genes effect specific bodily characteristics.*

Q.   On a recent TV talk show, a politician used the word obloquy. Classy, no?

A.   I wish you had shipped me the politician's name; he or she deserves kudos. The word means abusively detractive language, and the *loqu-* part comes from a Latin word meaning to speak. We find that relatively rare *–quy* ending in a few other words: colloquy, obsequy, soliloquy, and ventriloquy.

Q.   Would you please explain verb tense?

A.   I can't do that in a short space, but at least I can point out some broad realities about the time element in verbs. As the chart below shows, there are three basic time slots (*before now*, *now*, and *after now*), but there are six variations. This is because a verb may contain more than one time element. For instance, an action may begin in the past and continue into the present (or even into the future), or it may begin in the present and end at some future date.

Here's a rundown on the six tenses:

BEFORE now <			NOW		> AFTER now	
Past Perfect	Past	Present Perfect	Present	Future Perfect		Future

Present: shows action or existence at the time of writing (*I hear static*), repeated or habitual action (*We exercise after work*), or general truths (*The earth rotates on its axis*).

Past: shows action or existence that was completed before the time of writing; it usually points to a definite or specific past occurrence (*I heard static*).

Future: shows action or existence that will occur after the time of writing (*You will hear static because of atmospheric conditions*). Signals: shall or will.

Present Perfect: shows action that started in the past but still continues (*I have felt pain in my knee ever since the acci-*

Answer 39   (A) adamantine
[Gk *adamantinos* of steel, like a diamond]

He was unable to endure the adamantine discipline
required in a monastery.

dent), or shows action that started in a more distant past and ended in a more recent past (*After a series of closings and reopenings, the store has closed for good*). Signals: have or has.

Past Perfect: shows action or existence that was definitely completed before some other specific past time; it is a double past time (*I had heard thunder before the storm started*). Signal: had.

Future Perfect: shows an action that will be completed by some definite future time. (*By next summer, I shall have completed this project.*) Signals: shall have or will have.

For a fuller treatment, consult my *Handbook for Basic Writers* (Prentice-Hall, 1991), ISBN 0-13-381898-5. It's out of print, but you can track down some copies by using the internet or by asking your friendly librarian to ILL the title.

Q. Why is a $5 bill called a fin?

A. Nothing fishy's going on. It comes from the Yiddish *finif*, five, which in turn comes from the Old High German *funf*. While we're on the subject of slang for money, a $10 bill is called a sawbuck, which is a sawhorse with crossed legs at each end, thus resembling X, the Latin symbol for 10. And a C-note is a $100 dollar bill; credit the Latin C, which meant 100.

Q. Is an apocryphal story the same as a lie?

A. In most cases, that's the way the word is used today, but there's a broader reality: the hidden or secret books, which is what the Greek word meant. Some books of the Bible, such as *Judith* and *Ecclesiasticus*, were accepted by Roman and Orthodox Catholics but rejected by Protestants, and others were proposed as inspired in the early Christian church, but were not accepted by church authorities (*The Gospel of Thomas, The Gospel of Mary*). The sects that accepted them gloried in the fact that they had arcane knowledge unavailable to traditionalists. Mainline Christians ultimately shaped the word apocrypha to mean of questionable authorship or authenticity.

Q. Is there a difference between getting somewhere *in* time and getting somewhere *on* time?

A. Yes, there can be a difference worth observing. "On time" implies that there is a known schedule and that it has been observed: *We arrived at the airport on time*. The person was prompt. "In time" can imply less control or some degree of luck: *We arrived at the airport in time to say goodbye before he boarded his plan*. The situation was fortuitous.

Q. This one makes me grind my teeth: "The railroad station rehabilitation fund has already reached the halfway mark." Only people get rehabilitated!

A. Careful—bruxism can chip your teeth. I've seen this usage, too, and I used to chalk it up to careless substitution for the word restoration, but it's appearing so often that it must be gaining ground. And more and more, you'll see rebuilt homes referred to as rehabs; this appears, in fact, as a secondary meaning in *Merriam-Webster's Dictionary*. So, along with you, I'll continue to refer to drug rehabilitation and building restoration, but we may already be in the minority.

QUICK QUIZ
40. Anserine is an animal adjective referring to

(A) snails   (B) geese   (C) insects   (D) parrots

Q. Are *amend* and *emend* simply different ways to spell the same word?

A. Since one of the shared meanings of both words is "to correct faults," it would seem so at first. However, an emendment is something that applies to books or texts exclusively. When you emend, you are editing. To amend has a much wider application. You may amend your opinion, amend a law, make amends for a crime, or amend the composition of soil by adding elements.

Q. Why does lb. mean pound? I've asked some butcher friends of mine and they don't have the slightest idea.

A. It comes from the Latin word for scale, *libra*, and the counterweight used to balance an object of that weight. You'll see the blindfolded statue of Justice in front of many courthouses holding just such a balancing scale.

Q. Why do we say *play it by ear* instead of play it by eye or foot or some other body part?

A. The saying has come to mean improvisation and on-the-spot adaptation, and it goes back to the ability of some musicians to hear a piece and then be able to reproduce it without referring to sheets of music. Ear in that sense was a substitute for memory. I suppose if the saying had started with artists, someone could view a painting, turn away, and then paint it by eye, a new symbol for memory. Anyway, keep your eyes peeled, your ear to the ground, your nose to the grindstone, and your hands on the wheel as you toe the line.

☞ BUMPER STICKER ☜
Every calendar's days are numbered

Q. I went to a Catholic grammar school, and one of the things the nuns drummed into our heads was the correct use of the articles *a* and *an*. These days, it seems that no one cares, since they write "a FBI agent" and other atrocities.

A. Most people make the mistake of relying on sight instead of sound. What matters is whether the next letter **sounds** like a vowel or a consonant; what it looks like is not a factor. So it should be "an FBI agent" because the letter F (eff) begins with a vowel sound, and *an* signals a vowel sound coming up. In contrast, we'd use "a union representative " because the u (yew) begins with a consonant sound, and *a* signals a consonant sound coming up. The greater problem for most people, I believe, is failing to use *an* before certain initialisms. So we'd have "a one-time offer," "a ukelele player," and "a European vacation." And there would be "an FCC official," "an s-curve on the road," and "an MA in British Literature."

Q. What's the correct term for someone from Michigan, a Michigander or a Michiganian?

A. That depends on where you go for your answer. The official State of Michigan web site <www.michigan.gov> has this to say: "The Web site of the Michigan Historical Center uses Michiganian. Michiganian has a long history. It is the term used for the state's citizens in *The Collections of the Michigan Pioneer and Historical Society* since the 1870s and in *Michigan History* magazine since just after the turn of the 20th cen-

---

Answer 40 (B) geese
[L. *anser*, goose]

Because the three tendons splay out on the front of the shinbone and look like the foot of a goose, pes anserine bursitis is also known as "goose foot" bursitis.

tury. But people who call Michigan their home use the word they like best, and there is no 'official' term."

Using the Google test, I found 7,420 hits for Michigander, and 909 hits for Michiganian. The principal objection to Michigander that I've heard claims that if there's a Michigander, there must also be a Michigoose. I'm not sure whether this is political correctness or its stark opposite. Another contender is Michiganite, which earns only 92 hits on Google, but which seems to be favored by the U.S. Government Printing Office. Call me anything but late for dinner.

Q. How do dictionary makers decide how to define a word?

A. For the most part, they study how the word was and is being used, and they report on that. They don't make up their own definitions; they collate what they observe.

When it comes to nouns, there is an industry-wide standard that goes back to philosophical principles of identification: first, place the object in an appropriate genus (category); then differentiate it by species (significant differences from others in the same category). Notice how the following definitions of *lion* and *tiger* start out the same (genus), but then go on to detail the differences.

Lion: A large carnivorous feline mammal (*Panthera leo*) of Africa and northwest India, having a short, tawny coat, a tufted tail, and, in the male, a heavy mane around the neck and shoulders.

Tiger: A large carnivorous feline mammal (*Panthera tigris*) of Asia, having a tawny coat with transverse black stripes.

☞ THE GAME OF THE NAME ☜
Damian came from a Greek word meaning to tame.

168

Q. I heard that the word *barbarian* was used by smooth-shaven Romans as a contemptuous reference to bearded foreigners.

A. There was a Latin word *barba*, beard, which shows up in our word barber, but barbarian comes from a Greek word (*barbaros*) which was an imitation of unintelligible foreign speech, as if we were to refer to blah-blah-ism.

Q. Where did the phrase *party pooper* come from?

A. This one's a bit difficult to pin down. It refers to a person who dampens the spirits of others by his or her disinterest or lassitude. Someone's lethargy or weariness can act as a wet blanket on others, especially at a party where the person sits aside, sullen and uncommunicative. *Poop* has several meanings, but here it refers to exhausted or worn out, as in *all pooped out.*

The water imagery here (*dampen, wet blanket*) is deliberate. A couple of commentators try to connect the phrase to the exhaustion suffered by sailors when heavy waves washed over the poop deck and they had to hold on for dear life. You'll find this suggested in *The Facts on File Encyclopedia of Word and Phrase Origins* and in *Loose Cannons, Red Herrings, and Other Lost Metaphors.*

☞   WORD FACT   ☜

Some words change their pronunciation simply by being capitalized. Consider the difference between polish and Polish, herb and Herb, job and Job.

QUICK QUIZ
41. Relating to fingernails or toenails:

(A) gnathal   (B) buccal   (C) crural   (D) ungual

Q. I heard you say that using context is just as important as using a dictionary, but I didn't catch the details.

A. Every time you look up a word that has multiple meanings, you must use context to decide which dictionary definition is most appropriate. You test the meanings one by one by seeing if they fit the sentence that sent you to the dictionary in the first place.

Using context to decipher meaning often makes a trip to the dictionary unnecessary. Context involves studying the ideas leading up to and following an unknown word. It demands attention and analysis. Watch for the following:

(1) WORD CLUES. The writer actually builds in a definition for a word and uses word signals such as X *is/means* Y, X *is known as* Y, *that is*, etc. *The metal tip at the end of a shoelace is called an aglet.*

(2) PUNCTUATION CLUES. Instead of words to signal a definition, the writer may use commas, dashes, or parentheses. *Lipomas (fatty tumors) are usually benign and thus not a cause for alarm.*

(3) SYNONYMS. Watch for equivalent terms, either in clusters or in a connected sentence. *Falciform swords were standard weapons in the Middle East. The sickle-shaped blade was designed to behead enemies with a single blow.*

(4) EXAMPLE. Watch for the signals *for example, for instance, such as,* and *like. Pain is a useful warning signal, but most people rush to relieve it by taking analgesics such as aspirins, barbiturates, codeine, and tranquilizers.*

(5) DESCRIPTIONS. Look for words that help you to see, hear, taste, touch, or smell. *Dylan was emaciated. His clothes hung loosely from his frame, and his arms and legs could have been used as toothpicks.*

(6) CONTRAST OR OPPOSITES. Watch for contrast words such as *but, yet, however, nevertheless, in spite of, other* and *on the other hand.* Watch also for negative signals such as *no, not, never,* and *nor. People in authority should be careful not to hire mendacious aides. Assistants who are not truthful will make their boss guilty by association.*

Q. I know that some word endings can help you to figure out whether a word is a verb or a noun or an adjective or an adverb, but aren't there any that help you to figure out the actual meaning of a word?

A. Suffixes simply aren't as useful as prefixes and roots in that regard. But I will mention three categories that help to establish a portion of the meaning of a word.

(1) Some suffixes designate a medical condition: -ia (*anemia, malaria*), -iasis (*psoriasis, elephantiasis*), -itis (*dermatitis, bronchitis*), -oma (*carcinoma, glaucoma*), -osis (*halitosis, neurosis*).

(2) Some suffixes point to a location: -arium (*aquarium, solarium*), -ary (*granary, seminary*), -ery (*brewery, grocery*), -orium (*auditorium, sanatorium*), -ory (*dormitory, observatory*).

(3) Some suffixes mean short or small: -et (*eaglet, islet*), -ette (*kitchenette, cigarette*), -let (*booklet, droplet*), -ling (*hatchling, duckling*), -ule (*ampule, molecule*).

Q. A CBS football commentator at the Sun Bowl described an oversized lineman this way: "He ran so hard he was left grasping for air."

A. Since grasp means to seize with one's hand, there's no way he could have done that, not even in the most severe Los Angeles smog. The announcer meant to say "gasping for air," to describe breathlessness or convulsive intake of air. Of course, if he missed his tackle with outstretched arms, I sup-

---

Answer 41 (D) ungual
[L. *unguis*, nail]

The ungual infection lasted for weeks.

---

pose we could say metaphorically that he grasped air instead of the ball carrier.

Q. Loved your show on Christmas mondegreens. Here's one you missed: *While Shepherds washed their socks at night* (While shepherds watched their flocks at night).

A. I do thoroughly enjoy the mondegreen segments, and Christmas songs are a prolific source. For those who don't pick up the program, a mondegreen was the name given to misheard song lyrics by Sylvia Wright, who misheard a Scottish ballad as *They hae slae the Earl of Murray, and Lady Mondegreen* (They hae slae the Earl of Murray, and laid him on the green). Here's a sample of what listeners have called in: *Rudolph the red-nosed reindeer had a very Chinese nose* (Rudolph the red-nosed reindeer had a very shiny nose); *I'm dreaming of a white Christmas with every Christian car I ride* (I'm dreaming of a white Christmas with every Christmas card I write); *We three kings from Orient Tar* (We three kings of orient are); *Later on we'll perspire, as we dream by the fire* (Later on we'll conspire, as we dream by the fire); *Santa Claus is scum in two towns* (Santa Claus is coming to town); *Noel, Noel, Barney's the king of Israel* (Noel, Noel, Born is the king of Israel); and *Olive, the other reindeer* (All of the other reindeer).

Q. Is it important to distinguish *beside* and *besides*?

A. I don't know how high it is on the importance scale, but in general use there is a difference. We use *beside* to signify next to or alongside. It is a preposition, so it is followed by an object: *We sat beside the flowing stream. In the photo, George is standing beside his wife.* We use *besides* to mean in addition: *It was too early for dinner; besides, I wasn't even hungry.* So to make the correct choice, substitute either "next to" or "in addition" and see which one fits.

Q. I'm reading a mystery novel and have come across the phrase "bend sinister." Sinister makes sense because evil is being threatened. Does the phrase imply that disaster is just around the bend or corner?

A. Not a bad reconstruction, but *bend sinister* is a term from heraldry. It's something that would appear on a coat of arms. Odds are that you're reading a British mystery novel. The bend sinister is a band that runs from the bottom left side to the upper right side of a shield. (*Sinister* means "left" in Latin.) It often signifies that there was bastardy in the family lineage, but there are exceptions, depending on nationality. There is also confusion as to whether the band should run from top left or top right. A definitive source (James Parker, *A Glossary of Terms Used in Heraldry*, 1894) says this: "As shields are always supposed to be upon the arms of the bearer, it is *his* left-hand side that is meant; consequently the sinister is on the spectator's right hand." One more reason why the rich are different from you and me.

Q. I've got a bet with my brother, and I need your help. How do you spell the sauce made from tomatoes which gets slathered on hot dogs and hamburgers?

A. Don't forget fries; some people can't eat them without ketchup, catsup, or catchup. A trip through your local grocery store will show that even manufacturers can't agree on the spelling. All three are in common use, and have been for quite a while. *Catchup* appears in print in 1690, *ketchup* in

---

QUICK QUIZ
42. The diagonal mark used to signify choice (*either/or*) and in internet addresses:

(A) dieresis (B) virgule (C) ellipsis (D) aglet

1711, and *catsup* in 1730. Some purists insist that it should be spelled *ketchup* because of its probable origin, the Malay word ke-chap, a fish gravy or sauce. Interestingly, in earlier forms of the sauce, vinegar—not tomatoes—was the common ingredient. Using Google, *ketchup* gets 850,000 hits, *catsup* gets 93,100 hits, and *catchup* squeezes out 81,400 hits, though many of those seem to be company names rather than condiments.

Q. Should it be two bagfuls of groceries or two bags full of groceries?

A. Either will do nicely. Notice that the first version contains a compound word (bagful). The general rule is that compounds ending in *–ful* (notice, just one L) form the plural by adding *–s* at the very end of the word. Thus, we have pocketfuls, shovelfuls, bottlefuls, armfuls, and so on. But when you use two separate words instead of a compound (bags full), the plural ending goes with the main word: pockets full of sand, shovels full of manure, bottles full of water, arms full of firewood, etc. Avoid putting the *–s* in the middle of a compound: pocketsful, shovelsful, etc. That's increasingly being designated as wrong. As for nuance of meaning, the compound throws the focus on the item contained; the two-word version emphasizes the container itself.

Q. If I'm writing a report that contains one or more lists, what's the proper way to move from item to item—numbers alone, numbers with periods, numbers inside parentheses, or numbers expressed as words (*first, second, third*, etc.)? I've seen all of these, and it seems a bit chaotic.

A. Some of the chaos comes from the fact that style books vary and conventions change over the years. Expressing ordinal numbers as words (*first, second, third*, etc.) is something I'd use in an essay or in a narrative account, while numbers written as numbers would be more appropriate in a business or economic report, a paper with a scientific bent, etc. When it comes to numbers with periods or with parentheses, I use *The Chicago Manual of Style* as my guide. It recommends numbers with periods for a drop-down list where each new item gets a new line:

1. Introduction
2. Body
3. Conclusion

When the numbered items are incorporated into a paragraph, the recommended style is to enclose the numbers in parentheses without a period: "Every essay should contain (1) an introduction, (2) a body, and (3) a conclusion." This works with letters, too.

Q. I've been curious about the phrase *swan song*. Where did that come from?

A. A swan song refers to a final performance, an author's last book, someone's last public effort, etc. It is based on an ancient legend that just before a swan dies, it breaks out into unbelievably beautiful song—this after a lifetime of silence. It became a standard image in English literature. Shakespeare, for instance, used it several times: "I am the cygnet to this pale faint swan, Who chants a doleful hymn to his own death..." (*King John*, Act V, Scene 7). " Let music sound while he doth make his choice; Then, if he lose, he makes a swan-like end, Fading in music..." (*The Merchant of Venice*, Act III, Scene 2). " I will play the swan, And die in music..." (*Othello*, Act V, Scene 2).

Answer 42   (B) virgule
[L. *virga*, rod]

The virgule stands for per in the phrase "55 miles/hour."

Q.   What's the difference between an archaic word and an obsolete word?

A.   Both dictionary labels warn you that the word in question may be hopelessly outmoded and should be replaced with something more current. Archaic or obsolete words survive because people still read the literature of earlier centuries and need to know certain terms. Try getting through the King James Version of the Bible without a glossary, for instance. Of the two, an obsolete word is dead. It simply hasn't been used for the last 250 years, and it survives merely as an historical curiosity. An archaic term will show up occasionally in print, often as a misguided attempt at humor. *Forsooth, that rapper really gets down, dawg.* Then there's the term obsolescent, which refers to a word in the process of becoming obsolete. Alexander Pope had it right: "Be not the first by whom the new are tried, Nor yet the last to lay the old aside."

Q.   Most of the time I hear you talk about the Latin or Greek origin of a word, but sometimes you mention the Indo-European language. Was that a later development of those classic languages?

A.   It's the other way around. Proto-Indo-European is an assumed language, a scholarly reconstruction of the great-great-granddaddy of today's languages. It no longer exists, and there is no direct proof that it ever did. Reconstruction involves finding related languages and words and then extrapolating what the original form might have been. The assumption is that close connections cannot be mere accidents; instead, they point to a common ancestral language. It's somewhat like constructing the missing peak of a pyramid by extending the inclined sides from the base until they meet at a projected apex. Researchers used to designate the Baltic region as the home of the Indo-Europeans, but recent studies suggest that it may have been farther east, perhaps in Turkey. In theory, it would have arisen about 8,000 to 9,500 years ago among Anatolian farmers. Experts look for allied words of family relationship (mother), basic numbers (two), and words that betray climate (snow), flora (oak) and fauna (bear), and so on. It's an ongoing linguistic detective story.

Q. Villagers were *impelled* to flee the earthquake or *compelled* to flee the earthquake?

A. Both words share the *–pel* root, meaning to drive, and that makes some choices difficult. There is general agreement that *compelled* involves significant external force, whether by a person or a thing, and that *impelled* comes from an internal motivation. The problem is that the internal motivation may have been implanted by an external force. In this case, I'd say that they were compelled to flee the earthquake, but they may have been impelled to improve their safety and their fortune.

Q. Spelling bees, quilting bees, and all the other kinds of bees: did they get their name from the social nature of insects in the hive?

A. That may be an added element, but the origin is much less poetic. That meaning of bee may have come from a variation on the Middle English *bean*, voluntary help given to a farmer by his neighbors. At any rate, the 19th century gave rise to all kinds of "bees." There were apple bees, chopping bees, hanging bees, house-raising bees, kissing bees, quilting bees, shingle bees, spelling bees, and spinning bees. To bee or not to bee became a practical consideration.

QUICK QUIZ
43. Nodding one's head is called

(A) nictitation   (B) nivation   (C) nutation   (D) natation

Q. In church, the words *thee, thou, thy,* and *thine* show up in hymns, but nobody uses them in real life. Why is that?

A. Once upon a time—thanks to Scandinavian contributions to Old English—our pronoun system was very complicated. A strange feature of language is that, unlike government, it gets simpler as it ages. The words you mention, along with others, were forms of what is called the familiar second person pronoun (the one spoken to). Each function of a pronoun—singular, plural, subject, object, modifier—had its own distinct spelling. We are now reduced to *you* (the only spelling for singular, plural, subject, object), *your* (modifier right in front of the word it modifies), and *yours* (modifier at a distance from the word it modifies). *You dislike Tom. Tom dislikes you. Your dislike is apparent. The loss is yours.* [A personal note: I remember my father still using the archaic *ye* as a plural form for *you.*]

Thou used to be the singular subject form (*Thou hearest my prayers*) and *thee* was the singular object form (*We beseech Thee, hear us*). *Thy* was the singular modifier to use right in front of the word modified (*Thy kingdom come*) and *thine* was the singular modifier placed at a distance from the word it modified (*For thine is the kingdom and the power and the glory*).

One more observation: just as the article *a* is used today in front of a consonant sound and *an* is used in front of a vowel sound, *thy* was used in front of a consonant sound (*thy leg trembles*) and *thine* was used in front of a vowel sound (*thine arm trembles*).

Q. What is the # mark called?

A. It goes by a few names. In telephone use, it's called a pound key. It's also called an octothorpe, and it can stand for number, pound, or a typesetter's instruction to insert a space. Depending on other contexts, it may be called a sharp sign, a crosshatch, or a tic-tac-toe mark.

Q.   My English teacher says that all communication is merely approximation since no two brains are exactly alike. How do you react to that?

A.   There's a strong element of truth to that as long as you don't go overboard and say that no two people can ever truly communicate because of these individual differences. Daily experience proves that we *do* communicate successfully, even if there are barriers and bumps along the way. Classical philosophers used to say that all knowledge comes through the senses, and you don't have to be a neurologist to discern that the calibration or sharpness of senses varies from person to person. The extent of one's vocabulary also enters in when one communicates. That's why the motto of my show is, "The limits of my language are the limits of my world." Also, notice that we distinguish two levels of meaning in words: denotation, which we share in common if we use the same dictionaries, and connotation, which must vary from individual to individual. Finally, this is such a well-known element of language that there is even a word for a person's individual speech pattern: idiolect.

Q.   On a recent vacation to my wife's home town, I noticed that the inscription over the town library read "PVBLIC LIBRARY." What's with the V instead of a U?

A.   Two things are involved. First, classical Latin used the V to represent a W (before a vowel) or a U in other positions. So the V *was* a Latin U in the word *public*. In the 19th and early 20th century, a tribute to Roman architecture became

---

Answer 43   (C) nutation
[L. *nutare*, to nod]

Nutation is a slight irregular motion (etymologically a "nodding") in the axis of rotation of a planet.

---

a sort of historical affectation in public buildings. (Do we show less affectation when we call a building a Centre instead of a Center?) Second, when you're chiseling something in stone, it's infinitely easier to use straight lines instead of curves.

Another duplication that you'll find in Latin is the use of I to stand for J or I. Thus, you might have ordered an OR-ANGE IVLIVS™ in the Forum.

Q. Do you agree that the internet is accelerating the deterioration of English?

A. First of all, I don't think it is deteriorating. It's always changing because it's a living language, but change is not synonymous with destruction. Does the internet have an influence on types and rates of change? Probably no more than the printing press, the telephone, or television. You didn't specify what bothers you on the internet, but I'll assume that it includes the invention of new terms and the ubiquitous use of abbreviations in chatrooms, blogs, e-mail, and so on. Both would be happening even if there were no internet. If it's slip-shod grammar that bothers you, take a look at newspaper headlines, letters to the editor, billboards, etc. What surprises me when I do research online is how grammatically tradi-tional so many articles and web sites are. But then, I avoid the drivel that clogs chatrooms and blogs. Nor have I ever watched a reality TV show.

Q. On your program, you mentioned that for us to read Old English, we'd have to approach it as a foreign lan-guage. Since modern English is its lineal descendant, why should that be?

A. First, other languages have subsequently added nonlinear overlays, thus changing the vocabulary storehouse. We might recognize some common words, but precious few.

Second, the basic mode of communication has changed because of the influence of other languages and because of the simplification process that took place in over 1,000 years of linguistic history. To give it a name, Old English was basically a synthetic language; it depended on affixes (short word additions) to make sense. In contrast, modern English is basically an analytic language; it depends on word order to make sense. To illustrate, let's contrast a sentence in Latin (synthetic) with the same sentence in English (analytic).

Agricola puellam amat means "the farmer loves the young lady." The *–a* ending on *agricola* tells us that it is the subject of the sentence, while the *–am* ending on *puellam* tells us that it is the object of the sentence. The verb, *amat,* can mean either *he loves* or *she loves,* so we have to depend on those other word endings to pin down in which direction the emotion is flowing. Now here's the important point: because the meaning is built into the words themselves, we can scramble those words in every possible way without changing the meaning one whit. *Agricola puellam amat, Agricola amat puellam, Puellam agricola amat, Puellam amat agricola, Amat agricola puellam,* and *Amat puellam agricola* ALL mean "the farmer loves the young lady." Nothing changes.

Now contrast that with the English sentence, which depends on word order for meaning: "The farmer loves the young lady" and "The young lady loves the farmer" are not at all the same thing. One party may not even know that the other person exists. And it gets even worse as we continue to rearrange the words: "Loves the the lady farmer young" is unintelligible. That illustrates the total turnaround in coding that took place as Old English evolved into modern English.

QUICK QUIZ
44. A biblioclast is a

(A) book seller   (B) book lover
(C) book destroyer   (D) book binder

Q.   Which is worse, a rebuke or a reproof?

A.   Both words involve criticism or disapproval on someone's part, so it's not a comfortable situation either way. However, a rebuke is rather harsh and unrelenting (its etymology refers to chopping wood!), while a reproof can be gentle or friendly, meant to educate as well as chastise. So if you have a choice, go for the reproof. Other words in the ballpark include admonishment, reproach, censure, reprimand, and the somewhat old-fashioned chastisement.

Q.   So, I'm walking through the produce section the other day, and I'm admiring the variety of berries available. Then it hits me: blueberry and blackberry make perfect sense, but boysen and straw? And what the heck is a cran?

A.   Berry good; you were paying attention. I must admit that I never thought about this before, so it's been an education. The *cran-* in cranberry comes from a German word meaning crane, the bird. My sources don't come up with a reason. Do cranes eat them? Does the bush resemble a crane perched in a marsh? Any grallatorial specialists out there who can help? The boysenberry gets its name from the American botanist, Rudolph Boysen. The *straw-* in strawberry refers to a straw after all. *The Oxford English Dictionary* suggests that it might be because the plant runners looked like straw, but it hedges by using the word conjecture. The raspberry may refer to its prickly, scratchy stems (rasp file), while the huckleberry probably started as the hurtleberry (small balls). A fruitful subject, indeed.

Q.   Is it true that words representing animal sounds are not consistent from language to language, and if that's true, why not? I mean, a dog's a dog, right?

A. Yes, there is a huge inconsistency, and there's a reason. When you try to turn the sound that an animal makes into a word, you are instantly bound by the rules and patterns of your own phonetic system. And yet a hunter in any country can accurately reproduce the sound made by a duck, for instance, if he just forgets about converting it into letters and concentrates on the sound itself. So, word and sound are not the same thing.

You mention dog in your question, so let's look at some representative words that try to imitate a bark.

Afrikaans: *woef*	Albanian: *ham ham*
Arabic: *haw haw*	Bengali: *ghaue-ghaue*
Catalan: *bup, bup*	Chinese *wang wang*
Croatian: *vau-vau*	Danish: *vov*
Dutch: *woef*	English: *bow wow, arf,*
Estonian: *auh*	*woof, ruff ruff*
Finnish: *hau hau*	French: *ouah ouah*
German: *wau wau,*	Greek: *gav*
Hebrew: *haw haw*	Hindi: *bho-bho*
Hungarian: *vau-vau*	Icelandic: *voff*
Indonesian: *gonggong*	Italian:*bau bau*
Japanese: *wanwan*	Korean: *mung-mung*
Norwegian: *voff*	Polish: *hau hau*
Portuguese: *au au au*	Russian:*gav-gav*
Slovene:*hov-hov*	Spanish:*guau guau*
Swedish:*vov vov*	Thai: *hoang hoang*
Turkish:*hav, hav*	Ukrainian: *haf-haf*
Vietnamese: *wau wau*	

[*Source:* http://www.georgetown.edu/faculty/ballc/animals/animals.html]

Answer 44   (C) book destroyer
[Gr. *biblion*, book + *klastos*, broken]

Buying old tomes and removing pages to sell separately will earn you the title of biblioclast.

Q. Is there a difference between *founder* and *flounder*, or can they be interchanged? And I don't mean the fish.

A. Fish or not, both words can involve water of sorts. *To flounder* is to thrash about, to struggle. It's something we do when we're in hot water and there's still time for recovery. *To founder* is to sink beneath the surface or to fail utterly— it's all over. A ship can founder, as can a marriage, a project, or a collapsing building. As nouns, a flounder is a fish and a founder is someone who establishes an organization: *The orphanage founder provided flounders to the starving foundlings.*

Q. What do you call words formed from first letters, such as FBI or NATO?

A. If the result can be pronounced as if it were a word (NATO, MADD, WHO), it is called an **acronym**. If the letters are separately pronounced as letters (FBI, IRS, ESP) it is an **initialism**.

Q. As an internet user, I know what an emoticon is, but where did the word come from?

A. For the uninitiated, an emoticon is a small icon composed of punctuation marks—for instance, :-) Look sideways, and you'll see a smiley face. It's used in e-mails and on electronic bulletin boards as a way of showing that the writer is kidding or upset or whatever the mood of the moment is. The word is a blend of EMOTion and ICON. According to *The Free Online Dictionary of Computing,* it was first used by Scott Fahlman on the Carnegie Mellon University online bulletin board system sometime in 1980 or 1981. Professor Fahlman says that it was 1982. In fact, you may view the original posting by visiting his web page reminiscing on the event, found (as I write this) at:
　　http://www-2.cs.cmu.edu/~sef/sefSmiley.htm

Q. I frequently encounter the term *Third World country*, usually expressed in a dismissive or contemptuous way. What are the first and second worlds?

A. I agree that the term is often used in a pejorative way, but it didn't start out that way. It was meant to be a descriptive term, a shorthand category, and was coined by the French writer G. Balandier in 1956. According to his divisions, the First World consisted of the industrialized countries of the West, and the Second World encompassed the Communist nations of the Soviet Union and Eastern Europe. The Third World was everyone else.

Q. I have fond memories of eating Spam™ during World War II; I actually *liked* the stuff! Recently, a friend and I were discussing the name itself. She says that SPAM stood for Specially Prepared American Meat. Can you confirm this?

A. Now there's a refreshing question. Most people ask about the spam that refers to junk e-mail, a term that was taken from a Monty Python sketch. For this one, I went straight to the source: Hormel Foods. They reveal that the product was originally called Hormel Spiced Ham. While attending a New Year's Eve party thrown by Jay Hormel in 1936, Kenneth Daigneau won $100 for suggesting the now-famous name. He took the *SP-* from spiced and the *-AM* from ham. So it appears that your friend heard an incorrect story. By the way, a word produced by combining existing words is called a blend or portmanteau word. Other examples include smog (smoke + fog) and brunch (breakfast + lunch).

Q.   I've heard you and Ron Jolly trading puns on your show, and I wonder if you have any favorites.

A.   Two of the best spontaneous puns came from Ron. On one show, I mentioned a book by Susan Cheever, daughter of writer John Cheever. Ron chimed in, "Let's hope no one calls her *under a cheever*." The other one shot out when I used toxophily (study of archery) as a quiz question. Ron deadpanned, "Wasn't *toxophily and carry a big stick* Teddy Roosevelt's favorite saying?" And some of the callers have provided groaners: *A backward poet writes inverse. Santa's helpers are subordinate clauses. When two egotists meet, it's an I for an I. A chicken crossing the road is poultry in motion.* Just grab it and pullet.

Q.   I was reading a brochure from this year's auto show when the word dashboard caught my eye. Is that dash in the sense of running, or dashing in the sense of handsome?

A.   Neither one. Originally, in a couple of Scandinavian languages, *dash* meant to strike or slap. (*Psalm 91:12* has, "They shall bear thee up in their hands, lest thou dash thy foot against a stone.") Dashboards first were used on horse-drawn wagons, and the word shows up in print in 1859. It was a board or strip of leather attached to the front of a wagon that kept mud and stones from being thrown up by the horse's hooves and striking or splattering the driver. When the automobile was invented, it was a ready-made word to apply to the structure in front of the driver. Come to think of it, antidashboard would be more accurate, wouldn't it?

Q.   My buddies and I used to say "that's duck soup," meaning something extremely easy, a sure thing. Now I wonder, why a duck and why soup?

A.   I remember using that, too, as in, "Fixing a flat tire on your bike is duck soup." The phrase gained widespread popularity when the Marx Brothers used it as the title of their 1933 comedy. [Trivia item: that title had already been used for a Laurel & Hardy two-reeler released in 1927.] Tracking down its origin, however, is a bit daunting. Many wordsmiths (Christine Ammer and Michael Quinion among them) simply say that the origin is unknown, though most commentators point to the first decade of the 20th century as its time of birth. Charles Funk suggested that it was related to *a sitting duck*, something very easy for a hunter to bag. Eric Partridge (*A Dictionary of the Underworld*) speculates that a duck sitting in water is already a kind of duck soup—couldn't be easier, since that's a duck's element. I like that, but there's no proof.

Q.   Isn't gregarious a synonym for clannish?

A.   In its secondary meaning, it refers to animal species that tend to move with others of their kind, which is a sort of clannishness without the negative overtones. In its primary sense, it refers to someone who is sociable, someone who steps out of his or her small circle of existence to mingle with others. Both senses derive from the Latin root for flock, *-greg-*. Other useful words in that family include aggregate, segregate, congregate, and egregious

---

Answer 45   (A)   an illusion
[Gr. *khimaira*, a composite monster]

The risks of war are real, not chimerical.

Q.   I wouldn't even wrap the garbage in the newspaper page which contained this sentence: "Rover's perfect landing enthused the scientists in the room, causing them to break out in applause and cheers."

A.   C'mon, form an opinion, why don't you? The verb *enthuse*, obviously a back formation from *enthusiasm*, has been around since 1827 or so, but it continues to irritate people almost as much as *hopefully* used at the beginning of its sentence. But I agree with you on this one, for a specific reason. Normally, *enthuse* is part of an intransitive phrasal verb (*to enthuse over* or *to enthuse about*) and it defines an external expression of emotion, an outward direction. Here, it's being used as a synonym for *excited* or *elated*, it has somehow lost its phrasal status, and it is oddly transitive (takes an object). That just doesn't sit right. The strange thing is, though, that it doesn't violate the theoretical rules of verb formation, so it may be its newness that jars us so much. Check back in 100 years.

Q.   I heard a judge on Court TV chide an attorney for his excursive remarks. What did he mean by that?

A.   It meant that Hizzoner didn't appreciate the lawyer's ramblings; he or she needed more discretion and less digression. It came from a Latin term meaning to run out, as in running outside the boundaries. That makes it a relative of excursion, a pleasure trip.

Q.   What do you make of this sentence, from a Sunday feature article? "Given their massive size, dinosaurs must have been fearful creatures."

A.   Fearful was the wrong word to use. Break *fearful* apart, and you'll see that it means full of fear, which would not be characteristic of the biggest kid on the block. The writer should have used fearsome, which means able to <u>cause</u> fear. That -*some* word part, in the sense of *characterized by*, shows up in awesome, bothersome, cumbersome, gruesome, and dozens of other words, and in all cases, the direction is outward; the effect is on others. Be careful, though. There are three -*some* suffixes, all with different meanings and different sources.

Q. When I read an old text, such as the Declaration of Independence, I practically get whiplash from all the capital letters that keep my head bouncing up and down. Why were they so much in love with capitals?

A. Let's take a look at a sentence that will confirm this: "WHEN in the Course of human Events, it becomes necessary for one People to dissolve the Political Bands which have connected them with another, and to assume among the Powers of the Earth, the separate and equal Station to which the Laws of Nature and of Nature's God entitle them, a decent Respect to the Opinions of Mankind requires that they should declare the causes which impel them to the Separation."

Using uppercase letters was simply a convention of 18th century printing. Notice that the words capitalized (except for When) are all nouns; that was their practice. Within a sentence, our practice is to capitalize only those nouns that are proper names. Aside from convention, it actually seems to have helped people read better, especially foreigners. Sometimes the same spelling is used for a noun and a verb, so if

---

QUICK QUIZ
46. Mental lethargy or dullness is called

(A) desuetude (B) mansuetude (C) hebetude (D) consuetude

the noun is capitalized and the verb is not (*Respect/respect*) there is an unmistakable signal. Additionally, there are some pronunciation shifts depending on the part of speech: *Digest/ digest, Bow/bow, Lead/lead, Refuse/refuse,* etc. Once again, capitals helped. So they weren't quite as arbitrary as it first appears.

Q. Did you know that alimony is an abbreviation for "all the money"?

A. Spoken like someone who's sitting there writing out this month's alimony check. Actually, it comes from the Latin word *alere,* to nourish, but it's used for more than food, as I'm sure you can testify. Alimentary, my dear Watson.

Q. In old documents, the letter –*s* often looks like an –*f,* as in fuccefs for success. What was going on?

A. Printers imitated a fancy script –*s* from earlier scribes, mostly because it led to pleasing letter combinations. The –*f* version of the letter also had a sibilant sound, and it was called the long or medial -*s*. We have to use the letter –*f* to represent it, but it was a letter unto itself, with a very short crossbar. The general rule was this: use the medial –*s* at the beginning of a word or inside a word, but use the small –*s* as the last letter of a word.

Here's an example from Thomas Paine's *Common Sense:* "Perhaps the *f*entiments contained in the following pages are not yet *f*ufficiently fa*f*hionable to procure them general favor...."

Coincidence or not, the same thing happened in Greek, where an initial or internal sigma had one form (σ), and the sigma at the end of a word had another (s).

Q. We live in kinder times. When I was a kid, an informant was called a stoolie. Now they have the dignified name of whistleblowers.

A. I also remember the stoolie era with its twisted "honor among thieves" ethic. Stoolie was short for stool pigeon, and it showed up in print in the mid-19th century meaning a spy in the pay of the police. It was a reference to the practice in hunting of setting a pigeon decoy on a stump (earlier called a stool) in order to attract birds to shoot. The word also existed as a verb. You could stool your way out of solitary confinement.

Q. Are capital letters and uppercase letters the same thing?

A. Yes, they are synonyms. Once upon a time, they were referred to as majuscules, from a Latin word meaning larger, while lowercase letters were called minuscules, from a Latin word meaning smaller. Capital meant principal in Middle English.

I find the origin of the terms uppercase and lowercase fascinating. In the early days of printing, the compositor sat at a bench in front of two cases filled with individually crafted letters. He would pull them out letter by letter, selecting the small letters from the lower (and closer) case, and the less frequently used capital letters from the upper case.

Answer 46 (C) hebetude
[L. *hebes*, dullness]

Too many school children display hebetude and sloth.

Q.   A guy in my office is always saying, "Borrow me your pen." How can I get him to say lend?

A.   How big is he? That's the first consideration. After that, perhaps a stripped-down rule will stick in his memory. Tell him that lending is done by the person who owns the item; borrowing is done by the person who temporarily receives the item. If he finds it difficult to say "Lend me your pen," perhaps you can get him to say, "Let me borrow your pen." Perhaps Polonius wasn't such an officious fool after all.

Q.   While channel surfing the other night, I heard someone use the word semiautobiographical. What on earth would that be, a half-finished autobiography?

A.   It sounds like it, doesn't it? Or an autobiography that was actually ghost-written. As it turns out, *The American Heritage Dictionary* defines it as "relating to a work that falls between fiction and autobiography: *a semiautobiographical novel.*" A search on Google reveals that the word has been applied to Ingmar Bergman's movie *Faithless*, Doris Lessing's *The Children of Violence* quintet, Ernest Hemingway's *A Farewell to Arms*, and approximately 6,000 other instances. Let's see: if the author hedges enough, it could become pseudosemiautobiographical, an explosion of prefixes.

Q.   On *Meet the Press*, Ted Kennedy said, "I have the utmost respect for both President Bushes." Shouldn't that be "...both Presidents Bush"?

A.   *The Chicago Manual of Style* makes "the element that is subject to the change in number" the priority in compounds, and I think the principle applies here, with a slight difference. While we can pluralize the family name (*the Bushes are going on vacation*), the word *Presidents* is the anchor in the senator's phrase, so I vote for *both Presidents Bush*. There is a precedent in a common literary designation: the Brothers Grimm.

Q.   The phrase *predrilled hole*—am I missing something, or isn't that an impossibility?

A.   I get your drift. If it's already there, why would I have to drill it? The word is legitimate, though, when you think of it as a hole drilled before it is actually needed. Predrilling is recommended when you're putting up molding so that when you hammer the nails into it, it won't split. *Preneeded hole* might be accurate, but not elegant.

Q.   What does the word *prohumanitate* mean? My daughter ran across it when she was filling out a college application.

A.   This one had me puzzled for a while because I accepted the caller's description of it as a single word. As soon as I broke it into *pro humanitate*, the mystery was solved. His daughter had to be applying to Wake Forest University, because that's the school motto. Evidently, writing an essay on "What the motto means to me" is part of the application process. A word of advice to applicants: whether you're applying for admission or for a job, learn as much as you can about the institution or company beforehand. You'll be a more attractive candidate.

QUICK QUIZ
47. To dulcify is to

(A) empty (B) lose sharpness (C) dilute (D) sweeten

Q.   If I'm ill, do I describe myself as *nauseated* or *nauseous*?

A.   Common usage is changing things, but traditionally, nauseated meant feeling ill, and nauseous meant causing illness. So a nauseous sulfur smell would make you feel nauseated. The word nauseating seems to be preferred to nauseous these days. Of the three, nauseous is the one most misused. If you say, "I'm nauseous," there are still enough people around who will say, "You certainly are!"

Sidebar: all three words came from a Greek word meaning ship. Surf's up!

Q.   My grandfather used to say "Little pitchers should be seen and not heard." Do you know what that means?

A.   I can reconstruct a meaning, though I never heard it expressed exactly that way before. Children used to be called little pitchers because their head and jutting ears were being compared to a container for liquids with projecting handles. The standard saying was, "Little pitchers have big ears," meaning, "Watch out— the kid's listening!" There was another saying, "Children should be seen and not heard." So it looks as if your grandfather combined the two.

Q.   From its prefix, shouldn't antipasto mean *against* pasta?

A.   I don't know when the spelling shift took place, but it actually comes from *ante-*, meaning before. It's an appetizer plate served before the main course.

☞   BUMPER STICKER   ☜
Reading while sunbathing makes you well-red

Q. I know that *seeing pink elephants* is a euphemism for being drunk, but why that color and that animal?

A. Actually, there are references to blue devils, red spiders, red monkeys, pink giraffes, and blue mice, too. But by the early decades of the 20th century, pink elephants were the symbol of choice. Perhaps it was the influence of Jack London's book, *John Barleycorn*.

Q. In a book, are a preface and a foreword simply different names for the same thing?

A. In general use, a preface is introductory material written by the author, and a foreword is introductory material written by someone else.

Q. Where did Rhode Island get its name? It ain't a road and it ain't an island.

A. In 1524, the Italian navigator Giovanni Verrazzano described Block Island as "about the bigness of the Island of Rhodes," and that name was later used by Roger Williams and the early founders. *Rhode Island and Providence Plantations* was the official name recorded in the state's charter.

The name recalls the Greek Isle of Rhodes, famous for one of the Seven Wonders of the Ancient World, the Colossus of Rhodes. It was a huge bronze statue of the sun god, Helios, and it stood 110 feet high. It is said that it inspired French sculptor Auguste Bartholdi as he designed the Statue of Liberty.

Answer 47 (D) sweeten
[L. *dulcis*, sweet]

A clove cordial may be dulcified at
pleasure with refined sugar.

Q.   Shooting fish in a barrel—where did that saying come from?

A.   I think it was an American hyperbolized adaptation of *shooting ducks in a pond*, both of which would be very unsportsmanlike. *To shoot flying* appeared in print in 1698 as praise for sportsmanlike conduct; the birds were in flight. *To shoot sitting* was its opposite, and it was said with contempt.

Q.   The expression meaning impatience, eagerness to get going—should it be champing at the bit or chomping at the bit?

A.   Champing at the bit seems to be older (it shows up in the 16th century), but it gets a run for its money with the competition. Chomping is a popular regional or dialectical variation, and on Google, at least, it's used more than twice as much as champing. So both will work. The expression started as a reference to a horse—the bit was the metal rod inserted in the horse's mouth and attached to the reins as a means of control—but it is now applied metaphorically to humans.

Q.   *Mad as the dickens*: does that refer to novelist Charles Dickens? I know he was upset by the social conditions of his day, especially child labor.

A.   It's difficult to pin down any particular Dickens, though that family name had an obvious influence on the word choice. But dickens is really a euphemism for the devil, and it shows up in other phrases: *What the dickens was that? My mother gave us the dickens for talking back.* Another mild, or minced, oath uses another *–d* word: deuce. *Who the deuce was that masked man?*

Q. I came across a fancy word for a boxer: pugilist.

A. Thanks for sharing. It comes from a Latin word meaning fist, and it also shows up in pugil stick (a padded stick used to train soldiers for combat). Variations are used in pugnacious (belligerent or combative), impugn (to assail), oppugn (to fight against), and repugn (contend against).

Q. What do you call it when letters are deliberately left out of a word?

A. That depends on which part of the word has been altered.
- Aphesis is the name when an initial letter is dropped: *alone* becomes *lone*.
- Syncope refers to a loss inside the word: *forecastle* becomes *fo'c'sle*.
- Apocope designates a loss at the end of a word: *going* becomes *goin'*.

Q. I'm annoyed by a mistake that I hear all the time. Years ago, an English teacher made it very clear that you can climb only one way: up. But I hear people saying things like, "Climb down from there." That's wrong, isn't it?

A. You had me worried for a minute, since I've been saying *climb down* since I was a youngster. I'm at a loss as to why your teacher was so adamant about this. The first few definitions do speak of rising, but in *The American Heritage*

QUICK QUIZ
48. Nugatory means

(A) unimportant   (B) lumpy
(C) caused by friction   (D) gently pushed

Dictionary, one of the examples is, *climbed down the ladder.* Even the venerable *Oxford English Dictionary* balances one sense (*to ascend*) with the other (*to descend by the same means*). It would appear that your teacher stopped reading after the first meaning, but when there are multiple meanings to a word, all of them must be factored in.

Q. Why on earth do actors say *break a leg* as an expression of good luck? It's all backwards.

A. Evidently, actors are a particularly superstitious lot, and this indirection is a way of fooling fate. They also don't whistle in a theater, don't read the very last line at a rehearsal, and never mention the name of Shakespeare's Scottish play, Macbeth. (*Oops!*)

Various explanations have been brought forward, including the strange notion that it's a reference to John Wilkes Booth and his broken leg. Of all the experts, Eric Partridge makes the best case when he says that it came into the American theater by way of immigrating Yiddish actors right after World War I. The phrase in the German theater was *Hals und Beinbruch,* neck and leg break. Worldwide, thespian superstition seems to be the norm.

Q. My grandfather used to have a standard line when asking the kids to do something: "If it suits your copperosity." Have you ever come across this before?

A. Not at all, and I despaired of tracking it down until I started playing with Google. To my astonishment, I found a website at <www.copperosity.com>. In those pages, a gentleman talks of *his* grandfather's dictum: "Green beans are good for your copperosity." Since both grandfathers in question were from Texas, we've found a connection. The website will provide you with details, but the source seems to be an old

Texas greeting that played with pretentious words. They were eventually picked up by Joel Chandler Harris and used in his *The Tar-Baby and Other Rhymes of Uncle Remus,* published in 1904. And copperosity was one of them. This is why I love the internet.

Q. I need to extract some industrial-strength words for *freezing* or *frozen* from an unabridged dictionary, but I don't even know where to begin.

A. That very same problem is what inspired me to produce my *Word Parts Dictionary.* Section II of that work is a reverse dictionary. You can look up concepts such as *freezing* and see if there are any word parts that bear that meaning. You'll find the combining forms *cheima-, crymo-, cryo-, frigo-, gelo-, kryo-, pago-, psychro-,* and *rhigo-,* along with the base forms *alg-* and *glac-.* Armed with those word parts, you can now look in the appropriate places in an unabridged dictionary and extract words such as cheimaphilic, crymophilic, cryogenic, frigorific, gelation, kryometer, pagophagia, psychrometer, rhigosis, algid, and glaciation. And if you have an unabridged dictionary on disk or on line, you can run a wildcard search and find those word parts even if they don't begin a word.

☞ THE GAME OF THE NAME ☜
Fraser meant strawberry in Norman French

Answer 48 (A) unimportant
[L. *nugae*, jokes or trifles]

Don't bother the supervisor with nugatory problems; take care of them yourself.

Q. Why do reporters speak of "the union rank and file"?

A. This is a military expression referring to soldiers and noncommissioned officers as opposed to officers; thus, it means the general membership as opposed to the leaders. The two words refer to military formation. Rank means the men and women standing side by side, right and left of you, while file means the soldiers standing behind you and in front of you. The officers stand up front or array along the sides.

Q. I'm curious about the phrase, "The life of Reilly." I know that it means in the lap of luxury, but who was the original Reilly?

A. There's some confusion about that. What is known is that it was a comic song that was a highlight of Pat Rooney's vaudeville act in the 1880s. It may very well be that the name was chosen because it is an almost stereotypic Irish name. *The Life of Riley* was a popular TV sitcom in the 1950s. William Bendix played Chester A. Riley, and the title was ironic, since he played a blue collar worker somewhat overwhelmed by life. His tag line was, "What a revoltin' development this is!"

Q. I was watching an installment of *Mutant-X* on TV, and one of the characters used a word that was supposed to mean fear of hospitals. I know it was a long word which had –*phobia* in it, and I'd like to track it down.

A. You're kidding—*Mutant-X*? And some folks say that TV *reduces* literacy. One possibility is nosocomephobia, which comes from a Greek word meaning disease. By association, it is applied to hospitals, as in nosocomial infections that are picked up by patients in a hospital.

Q. When we were young, my uncle used to refer to us as potlickers. Now I'm wondering if he was insulting us.

A. This seems to be a southern expression. Originally, it referred to the broth or juice (liquor) from cooked vegetables—usually from collard greens or turnip greens. By all accounts, when you broke pieces of cornbread into it, it was a tasty meal. So the word was spelled pot-liquor, but the informal spelling was potlikker, and that soon became potlicker, the hungry person who didn't leave a drop behind. It was a meal that would be characteristic of lower income families, so it was soon used as a synonym for poor. It also developed into a slur on someone's boorish manners at table. Finally, it came to mean an insignificant competitor. Where your uncle stood on that spectrum of meaning, I have no idea.

Q. Have you ever heard of an Irish bull? *The American Heritage Dictionary* defines it as a statement containing an incongruity or a logical absurdity, usually unbeknown to the speaker. "With a pistol in each hand and a sword in the other" is an Irish bull.

A. While I love oxymora and malapropisms, I haven't heard this term before—and my name is Sheehan! It gives me a new search term. Allow me to pass a few on to you.

- If Queen Victoria were alive today, she'd turn over in her grave.

QUICK QUIZ
49. alate means

(A) having fins (B) having feet
(C) having wings (D) having claws

- According to my best recollection, I don't remember.
- May you never live to see your wife a widow.
- Half the lies people tell about me aren't even true.
- Alone is much better together.
- At first, I had second thoughts.
- There I stood, thinking every moment would be the next.
- Deep down, she's really shallow.
- If your parents didn't have any children, neither will you.
- Looking me right in the eye, he stabbed me in the back.
- I'd give my right arm to be ambidextrous.
- Honk if you love peace and quiet.
- An oral contract isn't worth the paper it's printed on.
- I always like the same thing: variety.
- Focus on the unseen.
- It's unanimous; we agree on nothing.
- Once I get started, I don't know where to begin.
- They may decide not to make a decision.
- We were so busy, we didn't do anything.
- You are unique, just like everyone else.

Q. Why does *oz.* stand for ounce? Where did the –z come from?

A. There is general agreement that it came from a 15th century Italian word *onza*, ounce. That last letter may not have started life as a –z, however. *The Century Dictionary & Cyclopedia* says that "The second letter here, while identical in form with the letter z, is really the character used by early printers for the arbitrary mark of terminal contraction that is common in medieval manuscripts. It occurs also in *viz.*" That terminal contraction mark has a long history. It tracks back to Tiro, a member of Cicero's household, who developed one of the first shorthand alphabets.

Q. *A snake in the grass* is a very expressive term. Doesn't it refer to Satan tempting Adam and Eve with the knowledge of good and evil?

A. I can't exclude that image, although for centuries, Satan has been depicted as twined around a branch or trunk of the forbidden tree, not on the ground. But according to *Genesis* 3:14, the serpent was condemned to travel on his belly and eat dust, so that would make him a snake in the grass. The earliest secular instance of the phrase occurs in the Roman poet Vergil's *Eclogues* (37 B.C.). *Qui legitis flores et humi nascentia fraga,/frigidus —o pueri, fugite hin—latet anguis in herba*, he wrote: "Oh, children—you who gather flowers and early ground strawberries—flee this place! A cold snake lurks in the grass." As a metaphor, it came to mean a sneaky and stealthy adversary. And what a varied route it took. The metaphor was used by Dante, Anne Bronte, Mark Twain, Elton John, and a host of others.

☞ THE GAME OF THE NAME ☜
Donna means lady in Italian

Answer 49   (C) having wings
[L. *ala*, wing]

The feet of the god Mercury were alate to signify his speed and mobility.

Q. I often have trouble placing the word *only* in a sentence. Any hints?

A. You and millions of others. *Only* can be used as an adjective (*an only child*) or as a conjunction (*I would have stayed, only they told me to go*), but it's the adverb *only* that can lead to unintended consequences. The rule is that it must be placed as close as possible to the term it modifies. Check these examples to see how position affects meaning:

- Only my brother buys pork rinds. *[No one else in the family]*
- My only brother buys pork rinds. *[I don't have another brother — adjective]*
- My brother only buys pork rinds. *[He doesn't eat them]*
- My brother buys only pork rinds. *[Nothing else in the shopping bag]*
- My brother buys pork rinds only. *[Nothing else in the shopping bag]*

The most likely meaning is the first, so *only* is placed right in front of *my brother* to make that clear. Of course, depending on the brother/sister count in your family, the second sentence could be a contender, too; context would be the deciding factor.

Q. I came across a reference to someone's Ciceronian style. What does that mean?

A. It refers to an oratorical style perfected by the Roman statesman Marcus Tullius Cicero (106 – 43 B.C.). Thanks to an aide of his who developed one of the first shorthand systems in history, an incredible number of his speeches have been preserved, so it's not difficult to extract the elements of his style. They include elegance, lofty language, tripartite sentences (*we shall battle on the land, we shall fight in the air, we shall win on the seas*), the verb saved until the end of the sentence, and various rhetorical devices in the service of forceful indictments and parallel treatment. Modern style is much different; we must go back to American orators of the 19th century to capture adapted versions of the Ciceronian style in our country. Today, many would see it as too ornate, too indirect, and generally boring (*Like, I go, say it and sit down, dude*). Here's a quote from *Hamlet* (I.ii. 8 -14) that incorporates some features of the style:

> Therefore our sometime sister, now our queen,
> Th'imperial jointress to this warlike state,
> Have we, as 'twere with a defeated joy,
> With mirth in funeral and with dirge in marriage,
> In equal scale weighing delight and dole,
> Taken to wife.

Q. What is the most popular town name in the United States?

A. Interesting question. It takes us into toponymy, the study of place names [Greek *topos*, place, and *onoma*, name]. According to Russell Ash's book *The Top 10 of Everything 2000*, Fairview was the most common (141), followed in order by Midway, Oak Grove, Franklin and Riverside (tied), Centerville, Mount Pleasant, Georgetown, Salem, and Greenwood. Stunningly, the United States Geological Survey esti-

---

QUICK QUIZ
50. Able to hide; hidden

(A) palpable (B) ostensible (C) aperient D) abditive

---

mates that there are more than 3,500,000 current place names in the United States.

Also interesting are some of the strange names that may be one of a kind:

Blue Ball, OH	Boring, OR
Bowlegs, OK	Bugscuffle, TN
Dinkeytown, MN	Enigma, GA
Rifle, CO	Gnaw Bone, IN
Muleshoe, TX	Fleatown, OH
Accident, MD	Idiotville, OR
Monkey's Eyebrow, KY	Peculiar, MO
Good Thunder, MN	Unthanks, VA
Turkey Scratch, AR	Zu Zu, TN

Those wacky pioneers!

Q. I'm an intern, and my supervisor tells me that I use question marks where they're not needed. Can you help?

A. See? Your last question mark was fine. My suspicion is that you are not making a distinction between direct and indirect questions. A direct question actually asks something— it wants to know— and it ends with a question mark. An indirect question reports on an original question—it tells about a previous inquiry—and it ends with a period. Some examples will help.

- Did you see that cougar by the side of the road? [direct]
- She asked if I had seen the cougar by the side of the road. [indirect]
- When the fire broke out, where were you? [direct]
- I inquired where she had been when the fire broke out. [indirect]
- Have you seen our Neapolitan Mastiff? [direct]

- They want to know if we have seen their Neapolitan Mastiff. [indirect]

Notice that there are three differences:

1. In a direct question, at least part of the verb comes before its subject; in an indirect question, the order is reversed.

2. An indirect question is longer than a direct question because it adds tag lines (*she asked, I inquired, they want to know*).

3. An actual question (it asks something) ends in a question mark; an indirect question (it tells something) ends in a period.

Q. I heard your show on mondagreens [?] and I'd like to add to the collection. There's the misheard hymn, "Gladly, the cross-eyed bear," (*Gladly The Cross I'd Bear*), Creedence Clearwater's "There's a bathroom on the right," (*There's a bad moon on the rise*), and Jimi Hendrix allegedly singing "Excuse me while I kiss this guy," (*Excuse me while I kiss the sky*).

A. Thanks for adding to our mondegreens. Your contribution will go in the folder with Bob Dylan's, "Dead ants are my friends, they're blowin' in the wind," (*The answers, my friends, are blowin' in the wind*), John Philip Sousa's "Tarzan Strikes Forever," (*Stars and Stripes Forever*), Rod Stewart's "I used to love her, but it's Oliver now," (*I used to love her, but it's all over now*), Evita's, "Don't cry for me, Marge and Tina," (*Don't cry for me, Argentina*), and Crystal Gayle's, "Dough-

---

Answer 50 (D) abditive
[L. abdere, *separated* or removed]

The abditive nature of the heavy foliage protected the nest.

---

nuts Make Your Brown Eyes Blue," (*Don't it make your brown eyes blue*). Keep mishearing, folks, and keep them coming.

Q. I'm trying to remember a word that means very stubborn, even to the point of being obnoxious. It's not contemptuous, but it sounds something like that.

A. Let me suggest the word contumacious. It means obstinate, rebellious, and insubordinate. Having trouble with the kids again, eh?

Q. Where did the word *gimmick* come from?

A. Most authorities put this one in the O.U. file—Origin Unknown—but there is some speculation. In its oldest definition, it means a device used for cheating. Carnival and circus games, for instance, had many instances of spinning roulette wheels that the operator could stop where he wanted—at a cheap prize. Later, it came to mean any feature that would attract customers. It's also used to refer to a catch that may be buried somewhere in the fine print of a contract.

The Dictionary of Word Origins (John Ayto) suggests that at first it was spelled gimac, an anagram of *magic* used by conjurers. The Dictionary of Word and Phrase Origins (William and Mary Morris) offers two possibilities. First, it may have come from the German word *gemach*, a convenience. Second, it may be an altered form of gimcrack, a cheap and gaudy trifle. There is no entry for gimmick in the 1911 edition of The Century Dictionary and Cyclopedia, but it shows up as underworld slang in the 1926 Wise-crack Dictionary, and it hit the general public in a 1929 Saturday Evening Post article. 'Round and 'round she goes.

Q. Is there a legitimate choice between *disoriented* and *disorientated*?

A. Don't lose your bearings on this one. Here's the problem: we already had a word to express getting a sense of direction (*orient yourself before moving on*) when some asleep-at-the-switch genius decided to make a verb from *orientation*, thus creating *orientate*. It's simply not needed, and there's a general feeling that short words are preferable. So when you negate the word and use it as an adjective, make it *disoriented*. *Disorientated* is not only longer, there's a certain ugliness in the superfluous syllable. OK, then—which way is east?

Q. The weatherman on your station declared that "It's snowing in Cadillac right now," and for some reason I thought, what is *it* in that sentence? The weather?

A. Another deep thinker. The function of *it* in that sentence is to be a placeholder, a technical execution of the requirement that every verb must have a subject. The problem is that when we see a pronoun, we strain to find out what it's replacing. In this case, it replaces nothing; it simulates a real pronoun in order to give us the feeling that there is a subject and that all is right with the world. It's a type of shorthand for "Snow is falling in Cadillac right now."

Recall that the words *here* and *there* often serve as placeholders beginning a sentence: "There is a fly in my soup." "Here is a life preserver." Neither one is the subject.

QUICK QUIZ
51. Which adjective is used to signify the morning?

(A) diurnal (B) matutinal (C) nocturnal (D) pomeridian

Q.   I'm an elementary school teacher, and without naming names, I'd like to share a few student bloopers with you. One little boy wrote about "Paper View TV," an understandable mistake based on hearing. A little girl who had visited San Francisco last summer with her parents wrote about "Fisherman's Dwarf." And I got a big kick out of this title for a paper: "The Superbowel."

A.   Great stuff! I collected a few over the years from my college students, so growing up doesn't put an end to the mistakes. Here are a few; following your thoughtful example, the names are deleted to protect the guilty.

- These buildings are invested with rats.
- The jobless have options. For instincts, they can learn new skills.
- We take our country for granite.
- When a public official dies, the flag hangs at half mass.
- Sharon has a quick temple; don't get in her way.
- A man gets very wick in the knees when he sees a beautiful woman.
- All eyes were on me as if I was someone from another planter.
- There was a tremendous explosion that caused all the old women to finch.
- He could barely walk without the use of his can.
- The little house had a living room, a kitchen, a bedroom, and a guess room.
- The senior class began to walk double-breasted down the aisle.

☞   WORD FACT   ☜

There are nine separate word parts to express the color white: alb- (standard white), alut- (leathery white), cand- (intense white), cerrus- (lead white), ebur- (ivory white), lac- (milk white), leuco- (pale white), niv- (snow white), and ochroleuc- (yellowish white).

Q. One of my pet peeves is finding negatives used carelessly in a sentence. I've seen, "All electric shocks will not hurt you," "All men are not bald," and "Everyone's not a college graduate."

A. Absolutely illogical. These writers ended up saying the opposite of what they meant, in effect telling us that it's safe to stick a wet finger in the outlet, that there is absolutely no market for toupees, and that colleges may as well shut their doors. As always, the advice is to place modifiers of any kind as close as possible to the word that they modify. "Not all" and "Not everyone" will clear things up easily.

Q. Where does the word jackpot come from?

A. There seems to be no doubt that it's a term originating from the game of poker, but after that, it gets a little murky. Both Chapman's *Dictionary of American Slang* and Morris' *The Word Detective* say that it comes from progressive betting where the players need jacks or better to open. Each new deal of the cards until that happens requires the players to toss more money in the pot (the area on a card table where the stakes are placed). What makes me hesitate to accept this as Gospel is the fact that there are dozens of varieties of poker, and I have found no written proof that the "jacks or better" type was the original. All bets are off until then.

Answer 51   (B) matutinal
[L. matutina, *morning*]

Matutinal exercise is a great way to start the day.

Q. This may sound somewhat childish, but it's really just a trip down memory lane. When I was a child, as an insult we used to point to someone and say "P.U." while holding our nose. Where did that come from? I know it meant, "You stink," whether literally or metaphorically.

A. Nostalgia, indeed; I haven't thought of that for decades. Harold Wentworth and Stuart Berg Flexner (*The Pocket Dictionary of American Slang*) say that it is an exaggerated pronunciation of *phew*, a term of disgust directed at a bad smell. They don't give a date of origin for the abbreviation. It seems obvious that *phew* was the result of onomatopoeia, since saying the word involves a curled upper lip and a nasal sound. *The Oxford English Dictionary* cites its first written use as 1604.

Q. A TV ad confuses me. It shows a woman in an electric wheelchair, and the voice-over says, "A short time ago, this woman was limited by her mobility."

A. I can see why you were confused. Her mobility wasn't a problem; the opposite was. The script should have chosen from any of these possibilities: *limited in her mobility, limited by her immobility, limited by her lack of mobility, limited by her condition,* or any other logical variation thereof.

Q. My wife says that the word Easter comes from some pagan goddess. I maintain that it comes from a liturgical simile: just as the sun rose in the east, so the Son rose in the east. Who's right?

A. If there's a bet, will I get a share? I remember seeing your liturgical reference; it may have been a quote from St. Augustine of Hippo. However, your wife is correct. The goddess involved was Ishtar, worshipped in Babylonia and

Syria. She was also known as Astarte among Semitic worshippers. That name was transmuted into Ostara as the cult spread to Europe. It came into Anglo-Saxon as Eastre. Since the fertility cult feast was celebrated at the same time as the Feast of the Resurrection, early Christian missionaries in Britain incorporated some of the features of the pagan feast, thus explaining our traditions of Easter eggs and the Easter Bunny. By the way, if you are glib enough, you might be able to share victory in a roundabout way. The word east is related to the Goddess of Dawn, Aurora, but it seems to have been one of Ostara's functions, too.

Q. Is there a word for the loss of a brand name? I'm thinking of examples such as aspirin and zipper, which once were proprietary names.

A. To tell you the truth, I didn't know that Zipper had been trademarked. A lawyer friend advises me that generification is the name of the process, and that companies will spend millions of dollars to protect their trademarked names. Given the assimilative nature of English, I'm not sure that companies will always win the battle. It seems to me that Xerox, for instance, as a lowercase verb, will soon overtake the verb *to photocopy*. Can the company really hit each casual user with a lawsuit? One interesting aspect to this is that trademark law seems to be effective when preserving a trademark as an adjective (a Xerox machine), but less successful with nouns and verbs. Have to go now; I need to google some reference material.

QUICK QUIZ
52. Doxastic means based on

(A) conjecture   (B) statistics   (C) religion   (D) history

Q. I know that a stamp collector is called a philatelist, and a bibliophile collects books, but can you give me a rundown on some other fancy names for hobbies?

A. As it happens, yes I can. A few years ago, I did a couple of articles for Barbara Crews and her *About Guide to Collectibles* (About.com). One of the articles contained a list of hobby names that I made up because they seemed to be nonexistent. (*See* http://collectibles.about.com/library/glossary/blglossaryhobby2.htm) The other article contained verifiable names such as the following:

- aerophilatelist: one who collects airmail stamps
- arctophile: one who collects bear figures
- cameist: one who collects cameos
- conchologist: one who collects shells
- deltiologist: one who collects postcards
- errinophilist: one who collects revenue or tax stamps (NOT postage stamps)
- ex-librist: one who collects bookplates
- exonumist: one who collects numismatic items other than coins and paper money
- fusilatelist: one who collects telephone calling cards
- helixophile: one who collects corkscrews < www.corkscrewmuseum.com>
- iconophile: one who collects prints, engravings, etc.
- lepidopterist: one who collects and mounts butterflies
- numismatist: one who collects coins, tokens, medals, paper money
- phillumenist: one who collects matchbook covers
- succrologist: one who collects sugar packets
- vecturist: one who collects transportation tokens

Q. I'm beginning to wonder if anyone still knows that *dice* is a plural form for the word *die*? I see people using *dice* as if it were a singular spelling.

A. Another word in transition, I think. While most dictionaries are faithful to *die* as the singular form, I have come across articles and talk shows where *dice* was used both for the singular and plural forms. Perhaps some of the confusion comes from the name of the game itself, where the word *dice* is correctly singular: *dice is a game of chance.*

Sidebar: Ambrose Bierce had some fun with this word in his *Devil's Dictionary*: **DIE**, *n.* The singular of "dice." We seldom hear the word, because there is a prohibitory proverb, "Never say die."

Q. I heard you talking about Irish bulls, and I'd like to call your attention to another category of mangled prose: messed-up clichés. Two examples are *butt naked*, which I learned as *buck naked*, and *it's a doggy dog world*, which should be *dog-eat-dog world*.

A. It's a sad comment when even clichés get mangled. I know of no word for that phenomenon except malaprop, but I've encountered them, too. The list includes *beat around the brush* (bush), *smoking mirrors* (smoke and mirrors), *fist and cuffs* (fisticuffs), and *lowest person on the total pole* (totem pole).

Q. I don't know if this bothers other people, but I think it's a confusing habit when people read a quote and fail to show exactly where it begins and ends. I'll give you an example. I was

---

Answer 52 (A) conjecture
[Gr. *doxastikos*, forming an opinion]

Doxastic voluntarism is the theory that belief is subject to the will, i.e. that we are able to choose what to believe.

---

listening to the evening news last night, and a highly paid news reader said this: "The CEO was reported to have insisted, quote/ unquote, 'My company has *never* denied responsibility for the accounting error.' This is contradicted by the court transcript." See what I mean? He ended the quote before it began.

A.   Great call. This is a problem peculiar to speech; it doesn't exist in print. The newscaster should have started the verbatim statement with *quote, My...* and ended it with *...error, unquote.* Or he could have used another system, such as the one employed at *Recording for the Blind, Inc.* When I was a reader there, it was always a *quote/end quote* sequence sandwiching the actual quotation.

Q.   Where did the word *booze* come from?

A.   It was a 13th century borrowing from the Middle Dutch word *busen*, to drink to excess. This means the story that it came from a 19th century distiller named E.S. Booz is folk etymology.

Q.   It drives me crazy to hear supposedly educated people misuse *among* and *between*. I actually heard a politician say, "Between Iraq, Iran, and Afghanistan, this country has its hands full." English 101, folks: *between* for two, *among* for three or more!

A.   I learned the very same thing, and my teachers were rather merciless when it came to careless choice. I think it's a distinction that offers a clear and unmistakable message in many cases, but there's no doubt that this is a rule in transition. And here's the other side of the coin, something we were never taught: that rule <u>always</u> was an over-simplification to make things easier on students. The reality, as *The Oxford English Dictionary* reveals, is that, "in all its senses, *between* has been, from its earliest appearance, extended to more than two." The OED goes on to say that "[*between*] is still the only word available to express the relation of a thing to many surrounding things severally and individually, *among* expressing a relation to them collectively and vaguely..." Examples of <u>bad</u> usage are then given that contradict the inflexible schoolhouse rule: *the space lying among the three points; a treaty among three powers; the choice lies among the three candidates;* and *to insert a needle among the closed petals of a flower* are to be avoided. Substitute *between* instead, we are told. So I think you may want to lighten up, unless simplistic rules act as a necessary coping mechanism for you. I know it's difficult to believe, but some of the rules that English teachers hammered into our heads were nothing short of grammar superstitions.

Q. This may sound a bit crude, but is there a technical term for nosepicking?

A. You mean like going through a proboscis catalogue at your plastic surgeon's office? No, I guess you mean booger mining, as my granddaughter calls it. Believe it or not, there is such a word. It may be an imaginative creation, but an article actually appeared in Volume 62 (2001) of the *Journal of Clinical Psychiatry* using the word in its title: *A Preliminary Survey of Rhinotillexomania in an Adolescent Sample* by Chittaranjan Andrade, M.D., and B. S. Srihari, M.B.B.S. Their conclusion was, "Nose picking is common in adolescents." No scientific study needed; just look under any school desk.

QUICK QUIZ
53. alacrity means

(A) incompleteness (B) sadness
(C) eagerness (D) truthfulness

A fixated publication, that *Journal of Clinical Psychiatry*. It had already run an article in Volume 56, (1995), entitled *Rhinotillexomania: psychiatric disorder or habit?* by J.W. Jefferson and T.D. Thompson. Nothing on amychopygomania, though.

Q. Why do people say *has gone missing* instead of just plain *is missing*?

A. I remember reading somewhere that it's a British transplant, and some people still suffer the delusion that British English is somehow more prestigious. Try to stay away from *turned up missing*, which qualifies as an oxymoron.

Q. I was watching a Dracula film the other night (guilty pleasures!) and for the first time it struck me that when Count Dracula introduced himself as Alucard, he was disguising his name by saying it backwards. Does this practice have a name?

A. The first time I heard of this, it involved two aging college roommates greeting each other sorority fashion as Adnohr and Nasus. Innocent bystander though I was, my designation became Ekim. I found out a few years later that ananym is the term for this strange practice. In addition to being a form of disguise, a pseudonym, it is sometimes used by authors who love wordplay. Samuel Butler's *Erewhon* (1871) was *Nowhere* under cover. And a very curious ananym came into the language through jailbirds. They would refer to a *neves stretch*, meaning a seven-year sentence. (Source: *A Dictionary of the Underworld*, by Eric Partridge)

☞ ALSO KNOWN AS ☜
steep: to place in liquid to flavor it, as tea

Q.   I know that the word autumnal is an adjective referring to the fall season, but are there fancy adjectives for the other seasons?

A.   Yes, there are. Estival (also spelled aestival) is the adjective for summer. Hibernal, hiemal, and brumal all refer to winter, and vernal is used for the spring. Why winter predominates, I don't know. You'd think that summer would be favored.

Q.   It seems to me that dictionaries don't do a very good job defining colors. For instance, mauve is defined as "a moderate grayish violet to moderate reddish purple." And ecru comes out as, "a grayish to pale yellow or light grayish-yellow brown." That doesn't help me at all.

A.   You have an excellent point, but remember that when it comes to color, dictionaries are limited to using words for what is basically a visual experience. Notice that the primary colors are defined by using wavelengths; dictionaries try to find words for the derivative colors. The best way I know to identify color is to use a color chart. For instance, http://www.oreilly.com/catalog/wdnut/excerpt/color_names.html will show you the 140 colors decipherable by Netscape and Explorer.

When I was working on the Color Category section of my *Word Parts Dictionary*, I learned how tricky it can get. Since the word part *glauc-* was tied in to the color of the sea, *glaucous* could mean silver, gray, olive, blue, grayish-green, blu-

---

Answer 53 (C) eagerness
[L. *alacer*, lively]

He responded with alacrity, and the deal was
sealed overnight.

---

ish-gray, and a host of other permutations. I think we should cut dictionary makers some slack on this one.

Q.   I have enjoyed your recent shows on strange town names, and I'd like to add a few of my own. My atlas contains Muleshoe, TX, Virgin, UT, Slaughter Beach, DE, and Rocky Ripple, IN.

A.   Thanks for the contribution. Those shows on toponymy [Greek *topos*, place, and *onoma*, name] elicited dozens of calls during air time, and all kinds of e-mail. For the sake of equity, let me report one name from each state.

AL: Burnt Corn
AK: Eek
AZ: Horse Thief
AR: Toad Suck
CA: Weed
CO: Last Chance
CT: Giant Neck
DE: Slaughter Beach
FL: Picnic
GA: Experiment
HI: Volcano
ID: Hellhole
IL: Oblong
IN: Santa Claus
IA: What Cheer
KS: Speed
KY: Rabbit Hash
LA: Waterproof
ME: Purgatory
MD: Mousetown
MA: Sandwich
MI: Hell
MN: Sleepy Eye

MS: Hot Coffee
MO: Tightwad
MT: Joe
NE: Magnet
NV: Jackpot
NH: Rye
NJ: Cheesequake
NM: Truth or Consequences
NY: Horseheads
NC: Lizard Lick
ND: Beach
OH: Mudsock
OK: Greasy
OR: Talent
PA: Intercourse
RI: Tarbox Corner
SC: Coward
SD: Tea
TN: Soddy Daisy
TX: Cut and Shoot
UT: Helper
VT: Satan's Kingdom
VA: Lick Fork
WA: Humptulips
WV: Left Hand
WI: Disco
WY: Chugwater

I can't promise that these aren't apocryphal stories, but two of the towns above appeared in unintentionally hilari-

---

QUICK QUIZ
54. to renounce or give up:

(A) denigrate   (B) serrate   (C) prevaricate   (D) abnegate

---

ous headlines. A paper in Waterproof, Louisiana, is said to have carried this headline for a tragic story: *Waterproof Men Drown*. And in Illinois, not too far from the farming community of Oblong, there is a city named Normal. A society section headline read, *Normal Man Marries Oblong Woman*.

Q.   Since the word lease is the core word, why do we use the terms lessor and lessee instead of leasor/leasee?

A.   The problem here is that lease is the latecomer of the three. The original Anglo-Norman word was *lesser*, to lease, making the core *less-*. The *–or* suffix designates someone who performs an action, and the *–ee* suffix indicates the recipient.

Q.   Would you tell me if this quote by President Bush (*Meet the Press*) is correct? "There is a lot of investigations going on."

A.   "There <u>are</u>" is the correct form. This needs some explanation because two hidden factors are involved. First, the words *here* and *there*, when they begin a sentence, cause confusion if you mistake them for subjects. They are merely placeholders (technical name, *expletives*) to make the sentence sound balanced. The problem is that they require you to say or write the verb <u>before</u> you say or write the subject, which reverses the normal process. Particularly in speaking, a person may choose the wrong verb number. In writing, however, good editing should catch the error.

The trick is to find the real subject of the sentence. Technically, it is *lot*, which sounds singular, but in this case we must ask, a lot of what? Normally, a prepositional phrase does not influence subject-verb agreement, but it does when it's attached to quantity nouns such as *a lot, most, half, some, none*, etc. So, we'd say *There is a lot of skin showing at the beach* and

There are a lot of investigations going on. Both are correct because both are influenced by the accompanying prepositional phrase (*of skin/of investigations*).

The usual subject-verb agreement rule applies here (*a singular subject takes a singular verb and a plural subject takes a plural verb*), but the inverted word order and the qualified nature of the subject make it a bit more difficult than usual.

Q. Which letters of the alphabet look the same upside down?

A. I'm willing to bet that there's a contest going on with this as a question. In the past week, five different people have e-mailed this question to me. Listen up, folks: if you win, you have to cut me in on the action. The capital letters that are identical upside down are H, I, N, O, S, X, and Z. In lower case, it would be o, s, x, and z.

Q. On an internet bulletin board, I found this posting from someone at Ball State University: "Doubling the *i* in the words you site is a type of error called a hypercorrection."

A. You don't indicate whether the writer was a student or a teacher, but the problem remains: site should have been spelled cite, meaning to bring forward as an example. Cite is the verb form of citation, and it comes from the Latin *citare*, to summon. Site is usually a noun, though architects

---

Answer 54 (D) abnegate
[L. *ab*, away, *and megare*, to deny]

Someone seeking spiritual perfection must abnegate the luxuries of life.

---

and builders use it as a verb meaning to locate. It comes from the Latin *situs*, a place or position.

Q.   I've noticed that I'm not as fast as my classmates when it comes to looking up a word in the dictionary. They get to the word way before me. Do you have any suggestions?

A.   If you need to, review the alphabetical sequence until it is second nature. In fact, try reciting the alphabet backwards as an exercise. The reason I stress this is because when you look for a word in the dictionary, you will use alphabetical order three times.

•   First, you use the alphabet to find the section that contains all the entries beginning with the same first letter as the word for which you are looking. Think of the dictionary as being divided roughly into three booklets: A to E, F to O, and P to Z. Never begin your search on the first page and plow through everything. Open the book only to the appropriate third.

•   Second, you use the alphabet to find the page on which your word appears. Now that you are in the correct section, you need to find only one page. To do it quickly, use the guidewords, the two words printed in boldface at the top of each dictionary page. The left guideword indicates the first entry on that page; the right guideword shows the last word to appear on that page. Don't waste time looking down the page. Skim read only the guidewords at the top of the pages. So, for instance, you'd find the word *coupon* on a page with the guidewords **countless/course**, and the word *jaundice* on a page headed by **jargon/jeans**.

•   Third, once you are on the appropriate page thanks to the guidewords, you use the alphabet yet again to find the exact word you seek. All the entries on every page are arranged alphabetically letter by letter from the beginning of each word to its end. You will find it useful to read what your Dictionary Guide has to say about any peculiar alphabetical arrangement; you'll find it in the front of your dictionary.

Q.   Why is a fraternity or sorority initiation called a hazing?

A.   Rest assured that it has nothing to do with the weather. Instead, it comes from the Old French *hazer*, to annoy, pinch, insult, and goad. In the 17th century, it meant to scare or to punish by blows. By the middle of the 19th century, it was associated with the "cruel and brutal horseplay of American students" (*Oxford English Dictionary*).

Q.   I take the phrase *feet of clay* to mean having a weakness or being vulnerable (similar to an Achilles' heel), but where did it come from?

A.   This one originates in the *Book of Daniel*. King Nebuchadnezzar saw, in a dream, a statue with a head of gold, breast and arms of silver, belly and thighs of brass, legs of iron, and feet partly iron and partly clay. Daniel interpreted this to mean that even though the kingdom was awesome in its power, it would eventually crumble, like the statue.

QUICK QUIZ
55. fissile means:

(A) easily split   (B) belligerent
(C) hollow   (D) stationary

Q. Could you say something about the difference between *accept* and *except*?

A. As the caller went on to say, even newspapers are not immune to mixing them up. Think of *accept* as a positive word, one that indicates receiving or including, and *except* as a negative word, one that indicates leaving something out. *I accept your explanation except for the part about the flying saucer. Accept* is always a verb. *Except* can be a preposition (*everyone except Tom*), a conjunction (*I would buy the car except that it's too expensive*), or a verb (*An admission fee is usually charged, but children are excepted*). In all three cases, it's easy to see the negative or exclusionary aspect.

There is no such word as *acception*; an exclusion is spelled *exception*. The word that indicates freedom from obligation is *exemption*. It seems that the most frequent error encountered with this duo involves wrongly using *except* in place of *accept*: *Are you going to except her apology? I distrust politicians who except gifts from big business. The Rotary Club excepted him as a member*. In every case, the verb should be *accept*.

Q. I was idly reading a coin catalog at my son's house the other day after I had finished watering his plants (he's on vacation), and the word exergue kept appearing, as in "delta in exergue." Do you know what that means?

A. An exergue is the small space beneath the base line of a subject engraved on a coin or medal. It usually contains the date, place, engraver's name, or some other identifying characteristic. I had one of those blue penny collection books as a child, and I remember that D stood for the Denver Mint, P for Philadelphia., and S for San Francisco. At any rate, the word is based on the Greek word *ergon*, work, and as far as I can tell, it may be the only word in English that ends in *ergue*, which makes it an oddity.

Q. I wanted to check on the meaning of the word kakistocracy, something I saw in a letter to the editor. I couldn't find it in a dictionary and had to call the letter writer, who defined it as government by the least effective over the most amount of people.

A. That's pretty much in line. The word comes from a Greek word meaning bad (*kakos*), and it's the superlative degree of that adjective. So defining it as government by the worst, the most incompetent, or the least qualified will get the job done. Normally, the -*kak*- letter combination is rendered as –*cac*-. We find it spelled that way in the words cacophony (harsh sound) and cacography (wretched handwriting).

Q. I know that the word **facetious** contains all the vowels in order with no repetition, but my daughter claims that there are more words like that. Can you help me meet her challenge?

A. I'd be happy to provide some of them.
Abstemious (*moderate or spare*), **abstentious** (*self-denying*), **acheilous** (*without a lip*), **adventious** (*rare form of adventitious*), **aerious,** (*airy*), **affectious** (*obs., loving*), **alpestrious** (*obs., mountainous*), **anemious** (*growing in windy conditions*), **annelidous** (*pertaining to a worm*), **arsenious** (*containing arsenic*), **arterious** (*arterial*), **arteriosus** (*prolongation of right ventricle in mammals*), **caesious** (*bluish-gray*),**fracedinous** (*producing heat through putrefaction*), **gareisoun** (*obs., garrison*),

---

Answer 55 (A) easily split
[L. *fissus*, split]

Certain types of crystals are fissile and must
be handled with care when polished.

---

gravedinous (*obs., drowsy*), **majestious** (*rare, majesty*), **materious** (*obs., material*), **parecious** (*proximity of reproductive organs in certain mosses*), **placentious** (*obs., complaisant*), and **tragedious** (*calamitous*) all meet the requirements. Remember that –*y*- is sometimes used as a vowel, so if you want to include that letter at the end, simply form the adverbs **facetiously**, **abstemiously**, **abstentiously**, and so forth.

To put your daughter on the defensive, ask her to come up with some words that contain the vowels in *reverse* order with no repetition. She may get **subcontinental** (*under a continent*), **unoriental** (*not oriental*), and **unoccidental** (*not of the west*), but probably only science majors know about **juloidea** (*insect classification*), **muroidea** (*rodent superfamily*), **muscoidea** (*the family of two-winged flies*), **prunoidea** (*a suborder of radiolarian protozoa*), **pulmonifera** (*pulmonata*), **subhyoidean** (*beneath the hyoid bone*), **subpopliteal** (*recess in the knee*), and **suoidea** (*pig classification*). And only avid readers of the *Oxford English Dictionary* will recognize **quodlibetal** (*pert. to a scholastic debate*) and **duoliteral** (*consisting of two letters only*).

Q. Should the phrase be *to the manor born* or *to the manner born*? I've seen it both ways, and it seems to make sense both ways.

A. When the phrase first appeared in print (Shakespeare's *Hamlet*), it was spelled *to the manner born*. Here's the phrase in context: "But to my mind, though I am native here/ And to the manner born, it is a custom/ More honour'd in the breach than the observance" [I. iv. 16]. He's referring to the custom of chug-a-lugging a toast, something he thinks better avoided so that Danes won't appear to be drunkards. Of course, someone who passes out from excessive drinking might be to the manor borne.

Notes

ALPHABETICAL INDEX

A

BIOGRAPHICAL NOTE

Michael Sheehan taught English classes for 26 years in the City Colleges of Chicago. He is a member of the Society of Midland Authors, the Dictionary Society of North America, and Michigan Writers.

This book is a compilation of questions and answers heard on *Words to the Wise*, a weekly radio program (Tuesdays, 9:00 a.m. to 10:00) airing on WTCM, AM 580, Traverse City, Michigan.

Sheehan is a member of the State Advisory Council on Aging (Michigan), the advisory board of the Area Agency on Aging of Northwest Michigan, and of the Bay Area Senior Advocates, a consortium of agencies and services which deal directly with senior citizens in lower northwest Michigan. In addition, he runs a web site for senior citizens which is sponsored by the Traverse Area District Library. It is called *The Senior Corner*, and it may be found at http://seniors.tcnet.org

Mike lives in Leelanau County, Michigan, with his artist wife Dona and with Rosa Rugosa, a Neapolitan Mastiff who enjoys a good manuscript from time to time unless she is caught.